THE PROPER GOLFING HANDBOOK

THE COMPLETE GUIDE TO TRANSFORMING YOUR GAME

...er, the best round isn't the one with the lowest score but the one you enjoyed the most

All the very best

REVIEWS OF JULIAN MELLOR
5* GOOGLE REVIEWS

Eamon Pickering
Julian changed my game and thought process towards the game.

Barrie Duggan
Julian has a wonderful way of explaining everything in a comprehensive, systematic but simple to understand way.

Stephen Bowman
Julian has a genuine passion to help golfers of all abilities and the knowledge to coach players at any level. Julian has a rare ability to put a student at ease instantly, his method of instruction is refreshing in what can be a regimented method of learning. Whilst Julian has access to state-of-the-art equipment his approach is far from the paint-by-numbers analysis today's coaches rely on. Julian promotes a smooth flowing swing in the Proper Golfing System designed to reduce the chance of golfing-related injuries; I would recommend Julian Mellor to players of all ages and abilities.

Robert Frawley
Julian's lessons are very helpful. He keeps it simple so I'm actually able to do as he suggests, and it's improved my game. Simple more natural movements that really work.

Diego Pérez
As a senior with limited flexibility, the easy swing has been a revelation for me to enjoy golf without tension and relaxed.

Matthew Bird
I have known Julian since 2019. His style of coaching and methodology is fabulous. He has transformed my game into a repeatable, enjoyable experience.

THE PROPER GOLFING HANDBOOK

THE COMPLETE GUIDE TO TRANSFORMING YOUR GAME

JULIAN MELLOR

With Tim Davison

FERNHURST
BOOKS

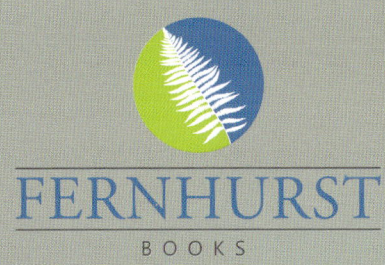

Copyright © 2024 Fernhurst Books Limited

First published in 2024 by Fernhurst Books Limited
The Windmill, Mill Lane, Harbury, Leamington Spa, Warwickshire. CV33 9HP, UK
Tel: +44 (0) 1926 337488 | www.fernhurstbooks.com

All rights reserved. No part of this publication may be reproduced, stored in a retrieval system or transmitted, in any form or by any means, electronic, mechanical, photocopying, recording, scanning or otherwise, except under the terms of the Copyright, Designs and Patents Act 1988 or under the terms of a licence issued by The Copyright Licensing Agency Ltd, Saffron House, 6-10 Kirby Street, London EC1N 8TS, UK, without the permission in writing of the Publisher.

Designations used by companies to distinguish their products are often claimed as trademarks. All brand names and product names used in this book are trade names, service marks, trademarks or registered trademarks of their respective owners. The Publisher is not associated with any product or vendor mentioned in this book.

This publication is designed to provide accurate and authoritative information in regard to the subject matter covered. It is sold on the understanding that the Publisher is not engaged in rendering professional services. If professional advice or other expert assistance is required, the services of a competent professional should be sought. The Publisher accepts no responsibility for any errors or omissions, or for any accidents or mishaps which may arise from the use of this publication.

A catalogue record for this book is available from the British Library
ISBN 9781912621750

Front cover photograph © Fernhurst Books Limited
All other photographs © Fernhurst Books Limited except:
P87: Woonsa57, Pixabay
P88: Jonah_H, iStock
P90: Pexels, Pixabay
P91: Kampus Production, Pexels
P92: ericlinus, Pixabay
P94: sisuhalland, Pixabay

Designed by Daniel Stephen
Printed in India by Thomson Press India Ltd

JULIAN MELLOR

Julian Mellor is a world-renowned golf coach and the founder of the Proper Golfing Academy, an online platform that helps golfers of all skill levels improve their game. With over 35 years of experience in coaching and playing professional golf, Julian is dedicated to helping golfers achieve their full potential.

Born and raised in the UK, Julian began playing golf at the age of 8 and quickly developed a passion for the game. Becoming a scratch golfer before he was 16, he turned professional at the age of 19 and spent the next two decades playing in various PGA competitive events.

After retiring from competitive golf, Julian turned his attention to coaching and quickly became one of the most sought-after instructors in the world. He has coached golfers of all levels, from beginners to professionals, and has helped many of his students achieve significant improvements in their game.

In 2013, freeing himself from the confines of being a Pro at a golf course, Julian founded the Julian Mellor Golf School to share his knowledge and expertise with a wider audience. Evolving into the Proper Golfing online platform, Julian now offers a range of courses and coaching programmes designed to help golfers improve their technique, develop their mental game and reach their full potential.

He has his own dedicated, indoor coaching studio and hi-tech simulator in his home town of Royal Leamington Spa, UK where he lives with his partner Jo Cameron, a former TV broadcaster, and their teenage daughter.

The author and publisher would like to thank
- **Copsewood Grange Golf Club** in Coventry
- **Nailcote Hall Golf Club** (home to the British Par 3 Championships)

and their staff for welcoming us to use their courses for the photoshoots.

CONTENTS

FOREWORD 8
INTRODUCTION 10

1. THE FOUNDATIONS: HOW TO ADDRESS THE GOLF BALL 12
2. THE GOLF SWING: BREAKING IT DOWN THEN BUILDING IT UP 20
3. WARMING UP & PRACTISING 31
4. THE CHIP, PITCH & LOB 42
5. BUNKER SHOTS 55
6. PUTTING 62
7. SHOT SHAPING 67
8. GETTING OUT OF TROUBLE 73
9. COURSE MANAGEMENT 83
10. THE GOLFER'S MINDSET 88
11. SENIOR GOLFERS 95
12. FAULTS & FIXES 101

APPENDIX
PARTS OF A GOLF CLUB 108
TYPES OF GOLF CLUB 108
GLOSSARY 110

FOREWORD

Golf is a never-ending search for the Holy Grail.

Anyone who plays this great game is constantly looking for ways to get better.

If you're among the most proficient you want to find the little things to become even more proficient.

If you're among the rest of the crowd you're seeking to improve enough to feel your game is more respectable.

Who out there doesn't want to feel better about their game?

Who out there doesn't want to hit better shots, handle difficult situations or be more effective on the putting green?

Where do we find the Holy Grail?

This isn't to say anyone can ever find it, but there is a way to come close, perhaps awfully close, to being able to look in the mirror and say, "I know I may not become a great golfer, but I know I am more satisfied with my game and have a sense of contentment and satisfaction."

Julian Mellor, a great friend and coach, has developed a plan to make that happen.

I first met Julian when he was part of the coaching staff for the late Brian Sparks who developed the Easiest Swing philosophy. I had gone to that website in desperation to find anything to help my erratic and inconsistent game.

Its foundation was simple. It was about the mechanics of the swing, how every part of the body should move in the process of a swing that takes a split-second to execute.

I followed it and I saw, not only improvement in the way I played golf but also, far more important to me, an enjoyment that superseded frustration during and after my round.

I now had an idea. I now had a plan of what I wanted to do, and when it didn't go well, I didn't vent, but knew what it was I should be doing. There's a big difference.

Julian has successfully branched out and developed a huge following with his Proper Golfing project.

What has made his approach so successful?

For one thing, he is immediately likeable. When you discuss golf with Julian Mellor you have the feeling he genuinely cares, his manner is calming and sincere.

I realise you can say that about most teachers, but there is something special about the way Julian imparts his knowledge. He will probably ask more questions of you, the pupil, than you will of him.

He has the innate ability to let YOU come close on your own to the solution of a particular problem.

He doesn't lecture. He engages in conversation.

His videos are clearly explained and if you are willing to buy into his suggestions and be disciplined to dedicate yourself to the programme, you will achieve your goal.

For me, he has been a good friend as well as a coach. The friend part comes first.

Now, Julian has put his philosophy on paper with *The Proper Golfing Handbook*.

The Proper Golfing Handbook starts at the very beginning with the basics of the belief he has developed from the days of the Easiest Swing and has taken to another level.

He is able to anticipate questions and problems for golfers of all levels, particularly seniors.

The Handbook deals with the various situations you will face on the course.

Everyone who watches golf tournaments on television has seen golfers reach into their pockets to check distances and other facts to know when playing each hole.

I can visualise all of us reaching into our bag to check on something in *The Proper Golfing Handbook*.

Now, we can put away the frantic never-ending search for a new way to swing the club and play the game that has done nothing more than confuse all of us.

The foundation of Julian Mellor's Proper Golfing approach may be all you need.

The Proper Golfing Handbook has it all.

Dick Stockton
Award winning sportscaster with CBS Sports, Fox Sports and Turner Sports

Julian Mellor and Dick Stockton

INTRODUCTION

Welcome to *The Proper Golfing Handbook*.

I have no doubt that you are passionate about playing golf and I'm certainly passionate about teaching it. I'm sure that together we can transform your game. The plan is to split this large subject into small, manageable chunks and describe them in words, photos, diagrams and videos. (Just scan the QR code at the end of a section to see a training video showing the technique.)

Most of the things you've heard about the golf swing are wrong.

I, too, used to believe in the idea of keeping the front arm straight, keeping my eyes on the back of the ball, keeping the lead foot pinned to the ground and holding lag in the downswing for as long as possible. I thought that the backswing should feel like coiling a spring and I believed tension made no difference to the way the body moves. The grip had to be perfect and anything other than the modern swing wouldn't work.

Well, how wrong was I!

In 2016 I met up with Brian Sparks, a fellow golf coach and author of *Positive Impact Golf*. We played nine holes at the Centurion Golf Club and sat down afterwards to discuss the golf swing and the way it was being taught. His thoughts were worlds apart from mine, but I was more than happy to listen to what he had to say.

Brian, who sadly is no longer with us, asked if I were open-minded enough to try some different things. I said I was and we moved to the practice ground. He got me to hit shots with my eyes shut. Hit shots looking away from the ball just before impact. Bend my lead arm excessively, swing my front foot past my back foot in the backswing and swap them over in the follow-through. To my astonishment not only did I hit the ball but I hit it so much better than with my normal technique and with far less effort. I was simply blown away!

After hitting about eight to ten shots (yep, that's all) I was convinced that there was indeed a better way to swing the club and I wanted to find out how it worked. I hit thousands of balls to discover the intricacies of the methodology and after about 6 months I decided to stop coaching the traditional way and help golfers discover their natural swing. I became an Easiest Swing coach, which was amazing, and later founded my own company, Proper Golfing.

This has proven to be a great decision and we now have members all over the world who benefit from the comprehensive video training library and one-to-one coaching. We also join together for fortnightly online meetings where we talk about all sorts of golf-related subjects.

When reading this book all I ask of you is an open mind. We are drowning in information. At some point we all need to stop making the swing over-complicated and awkward and learn to move naturally. The golf swing shouldn't hurt you and, when performed correctly, should not only enable you to strike the ball consistently but, more often than not, further than you are used to.

Have fun trying the different exercises and allow yourself time to perfect them. While doing so remember: we all hit bad shots but you can choose how to react to them. You can get angry or you can take the opportunity to learn. After all is said and done, do you really want to be that angry golfer nobody wants to play with?

Enjoy learning new things and I look forward to hearing more about your golfing journey when you're ready.

Kindest regards
Julian Mellor

Proper Golfing Academy – Squab Hall – Leamington Spa – CV33 9QB
Call: 07595 157 452
e-mail: Julian@propergolfing.com
Website: www.propergolfing.com
Website: www.propergolfingacademy.com

Note: I am a right-handed golfer, so all the photos and diagrams are right-handed. However, where possible, I have tried to refer to the feet as 'front' and 'back' rather than 'left' and right' to make it easier for left-handers. Elsewhere, if you are left-handed, simply substitute left for right (and vice-versa) as you read.

VIDEOS

To see a video of **Julian introducing the book and videos,** please scan the QR code

To watch a video click on the play button. This will allow you to watch the video on Vimeo, you may be asked to sign in or register (which is free).

CHAPTER 1

THE FOUNDATIONS: HOW TO ADDRESS THE GOLF BALL

If you can get everything right at address, you're halfway to hitting a decent shot. And well on the way to being consistent, too.

The set-up consists of several parts that all connect with each other. At the end of this chapter I'll show how they all blend together when you address the ball on the course. But first I'll give you more detail about aligning the clubface, the grip, eliminating tension, ball position, stance and aligning your body.

ALIGNING THE CLUBFACE

First some definitions:
- If the clubface is pointing at the target it is **square**
- If the clubface points to the left of the target it is **closed**
- If the clubface points to the right of the target it is **open**

At address, with the club on the ground, the bottom edge should point at 90 degrees to the target line. (Some golfers get this wrong and align the top edge, which closes the clubface.)

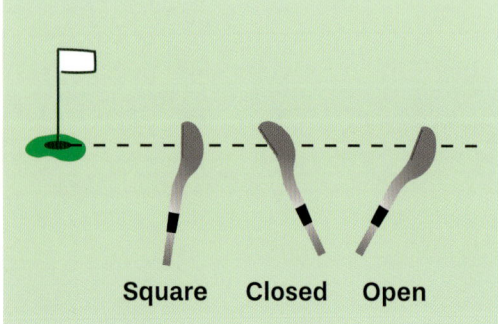

Clubface positions

At address, the bottom edge should point at 90 degrees to the target line

THE FOUNDATIONS 13

THE GRIP

The left hand goes onto the club first. The photo shows two points, the middle crease of your index finger and the crease by the pad on your palm. Place the club in your hand so the handle of the club runs between these two points. Then wrap your fingers and hand around the handle. From above, you should be able to see the first two knuckles on the back of your hand.

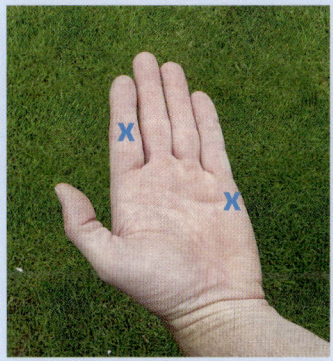

The club handle goes between these two points on the left hand

Wrap your left hand and fingers around the handle

You should be able to see two knuckles on the back of your hand.

The club is supported by the meaty pad of your palm. The thumb sits on top of the handle or slightly to the right-hand side so that it supports the club at the top of the backswing.

If your grip is correct, it should be possible for you to take off the thumb and three smaller fingers and hold the club just between the pad on your palm and your index finger.

Another test to see if you have the correct grip with your left hand is to take off your thumb and index finger and hold the club with just your three remaining fingers.

The left hand's thumb sits on top of the handle or slightly to the right-hand side

If gripped correctly, you should be able to take off the thumb and three fingers

You should also be able to take off the thumb and index finger

14 THE PROPER GOLFING HANDBOOK

The right hand goes on next. Identify the crease at the base of your middle two fingers, where they join the palm. Also identify the middle crease of the index finger. The club runs through these three creases. When the index finger is wrapped around the handle it forms a trigger finger.

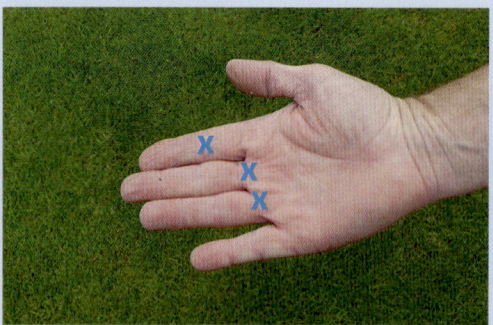

The club handle goes between these three points on the right hand

The index finger wraps around the handle as a trigger finger

There are three ways you can position your right hand on the club:
- The split-hand grip
- The interlock grip
- The overlap grip

Most golfers choose the interlocking or overlap grip.

But the best thing for you to do is to try each of them and see which feels most comfortable for you.

For the **split-hand grip** the hands are not connected to each other but the little finger of your right hand touches the index finger of your left hand.

This grip is good for people with small hands or not much hand strength.

For the **interlock grip** the index finger of the left hand is interlocked with the little finger of the right hand as shown below.

This is good at giving a secure grip which helps the golfer to control the clubface.

For the **overlap grip** the little finger of the right hand slips into the gap formed between the index and middle fingers of your left hand.

This is used by many golfers creating a single, secure holding grip.

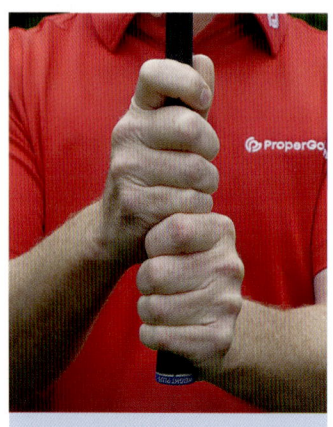

Split-hand grip

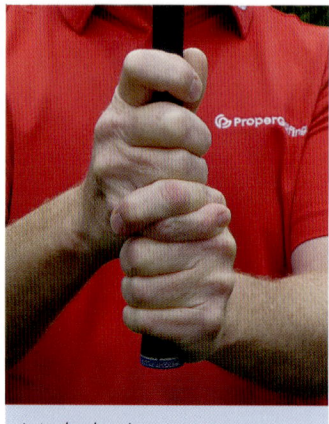

Interlock grip

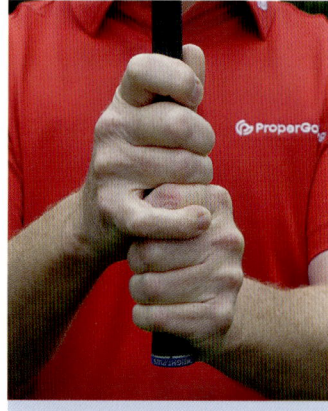

Overlap grip

THE FOUNDATIONS 15

Whichever grip you use there should be equal grip pressure between both hands, and this balanced pressure should be maintained throughout the swing.

You have probably heard the expressions 'strong grip' and 'weak grip', so I'll define them here.

If a golfer has a **strong grip**, it's as if their hands have been rotated clockwise on the club's handle – the back of their left hand points at the sky and their right thumb is on the right side of the club.

A strong grip is helpful if you want:
- More distance
- To stop slicing (a shot that unintentionally starts to the left and curves to the right during flight)
- To draw the ball (a shot that intentionally starts to the right of target and curves to the left to finish on target)

If a golfer has a **weak grip**, it's as if their hands have been rotated anticlockwise on the club's handle – they can't see any knuckles of their left hand and on their right hand the crease between their thumb and index finger point towards their left shoulder.

A weak grip is helpful if you want to:
- Hit the ball higher
- Put more backspin on the ball (so that the backwards rotation of the ball means that it is spinning backwards on landing and stops quickly)

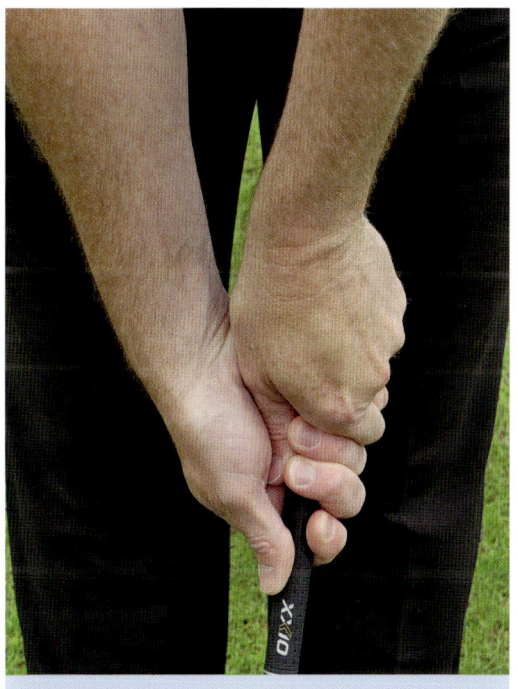
Strong grip

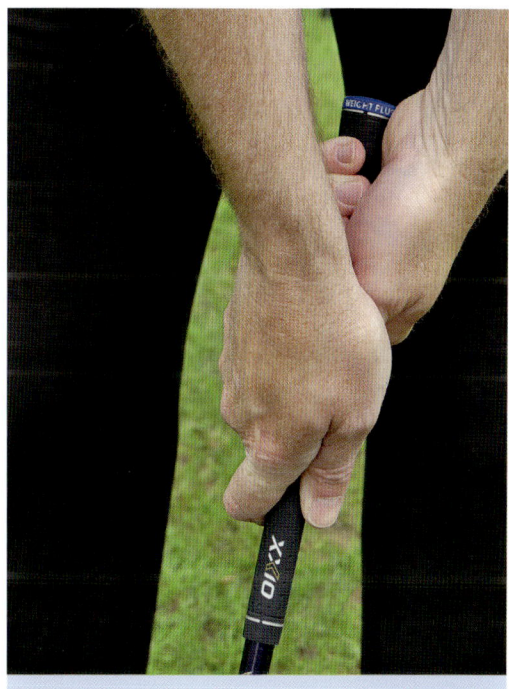
Weak grip

VIDEOS

To see a video of Julian demonstrating the **golf grip**, please scan the QR code

TENSION

How tightly should you hold the club? The answer is fairly loosely. If you were to score your grip tension out of ten, it should never be more than five.

Check this by gripping the club, then turn your wrists until the club is vertical. Gradually ease your grip until the club is about to slide downwards. This is the ideal grip strength. Now, keeping the grip constant, release your wrists until the club is horizontal, pointing in front of you. This lets you feel the right amount of grip tension. (Often tension increases during the swing, going from relaxed to tight, which slows down your potential swing speed and stops the natural flow of your swing, so should be avoided.)

1. To check your grip tension, hold the club vertical and gradually ease your grip ...

2. ... until the club is about to slide downwards – here it has been loosened too much and the club has slid down

3. With the correct grip, release your wrists – you should now feel the right amount of grip tension

BALL POSITION

Imagine the golf swing as a big circle. The bottom of the circle is in the middle of your stance and if the ball is there you are more likely to hit under it consistently. This works well with **irons from 6 to SW** (sand wedge).

For the **driver**, the ball is teed up so it should be further forward in your stance. Here the arc of the swing is starting to rise after it has passed the centre of the stance and we want to hit the ball in the middle of the club. The higher the tee, the further forward the ball should be, to a maximum of your front heel.

For the **5 iron**, **hybrids** and **fairway woods**, the ball position is between these two extremes.

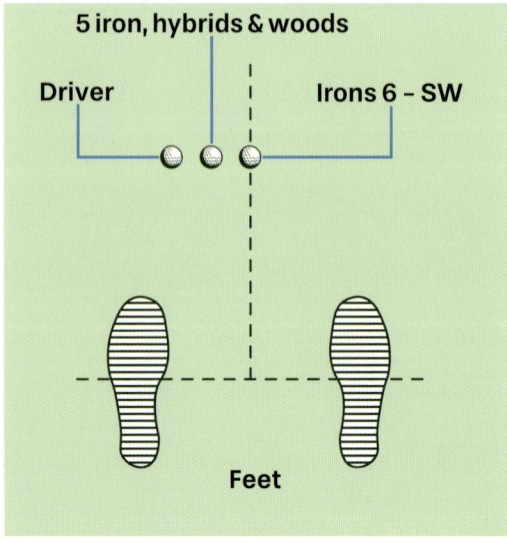

Ball positions (right-handed golfer)

STANCE WIDTH

The width of your stance is important:
- Too wide restricts body movement and leads to more of an arm swing
- Too narrow leaves you unstable

The best width of stance is your natural stride. To find this, face away from the target, keep your front foot still and take a stride with your back foot. Then rotate both feet to face the ball.

I recommend the following method to position the ball correctly in your stance:
- Face the ball with your feet together
- Move your left foot half a pace to the left
- Then move your right foot half a pace to the right

This gives a set-up with the ball central:
- For the driver you move your left foot less and your right foot more
- For woods and hybrids move your feet to give an intermediate ball position

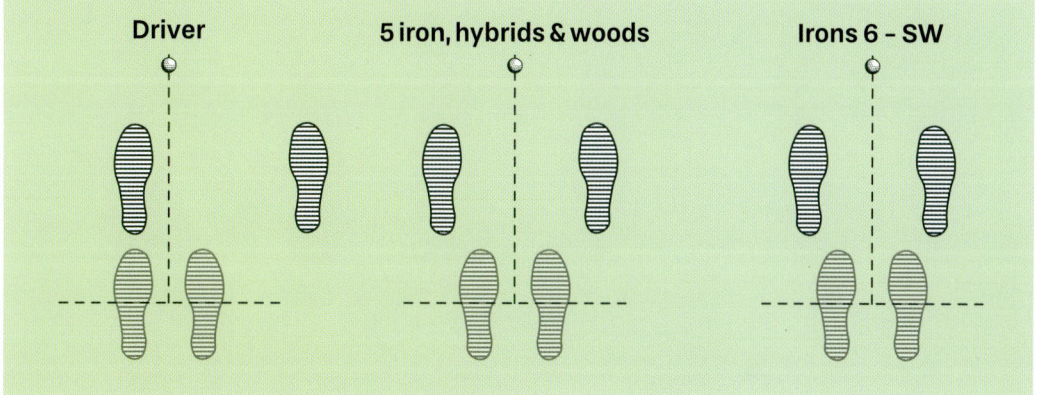

Move your feet like this to give the correct ball position (right-handed golfer)

BODY ALIGNMENT

The only thing that points at the target is the clubface, which is aimed down the target line. Everything else is aimed slightly to the left, on a line parallel to the target line. The distance between the parallel lines depends on the club's length and the golfer's posture (if they're bending over the distance is greater).

When taking your stance make sure that your feet (strictly your heels) are aligned parallel to the target line, then do the same for your knees, hips and shoulders. In practice sessions you can use alignment sticks to help your body alignment.

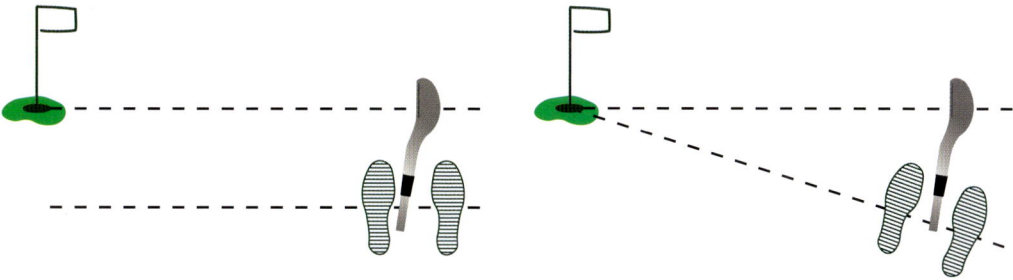

The clubface points at the target: everything else should be parallel and slightly left

Beware: if your feet and body are pointing at the target, their alignment is too far right

THE COMPLETE SET-UP

The idea is to set up using the same routine every time, which will help with consistency when you are playing. This will be a great comfort when you're under pressure or faced with a challenging shot.

1. Take a practice swing that resembles the type of swing you need to make to play the shot
2. Stand behind the ball and choose your target carefully
3. Choose the correct club for the shot
4. Take your grip on the golf club
5. Stand fractionally too far away from the ball before you set up to it and follow this sequence
6. Stand tall with your back and legs straight and your arms relaxed on your body with your natural width of stance
7. Keep your back straight and your legs straight and bend forward from your hips until the clubhead is on the ground
8. Soften your knees but avoid bending them too much
9. If you find the golf ball is slightly too far away from you avoid stretching your arms to reach the ball. Instead shuffle your feet forwards until your clubhead is behind the ball
10. Check that your body alignment is correct and that your front shoulder is slightly higher than your back shoulder due to your back hand being lower on the grip
11. Squeeze the club tightly for two seconds and then relax your grip. This creates an awareness of tension and allows you to feel relaxed just before you play your shot
12. Take a nice deep relaxing breath and you're now ready to play the shot

VIDEOS

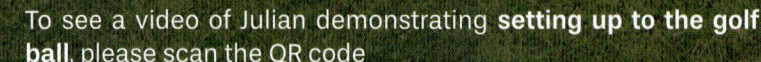 To see a video of Julian demonstrating **setting up to the golf ball**, please scan the QR code

THE FOUNDATIONS   19

1. Stand upright with your feet together and your arms relaxed on your chest

2. Keeping your legs and back straight, bend forwards from your hips so the club touches the ground

3. Move your feet apart to get the correct width of stance

4. Soften your knees but avoid bending them too much

5. If you find that the ball is too far away shuffle your feet forwards until your club is behind the ball

6. Check your body alignment is correct and you're ready to play the shot

CHAPTER 2

THE GOLF SWING: BREAKING IT DOWN THEN BUILDING IT UP

Now we turn to the much talked-about golf swing. Whole books have been written about it, but I hope I can help you improve yours in slightly fewer words!

The golf swing has two key parts:
- The **body turn** is the engine
- The **arms and hands** are the steering wheel

They are equally important and one is no good without the other.

I have broken the swing down further, into six principles. These are covered in detail below:
1. Turning the body about the spine
2. Weight transfer
3. Coordination of body, arms and wrists
4. Rhythm
5. Balance
6. Reducing tension

TURNING YOUR BODY

In the golf swing, the head of the club moves around a circle (The Circle) and this is on an angled plane. The angle is set at address from the middle of the clubface to the upper sternum. It's roughly 45 degrees but for a wedge the angle is a bit more vertical and for a driver a bit more horizontal.

Note that you **turn your body about your spine** to move the club around a circle (The Circle). Relax the arms and don't hit at the ball.

Turn your body around the spine

THE GOLF SWING 21

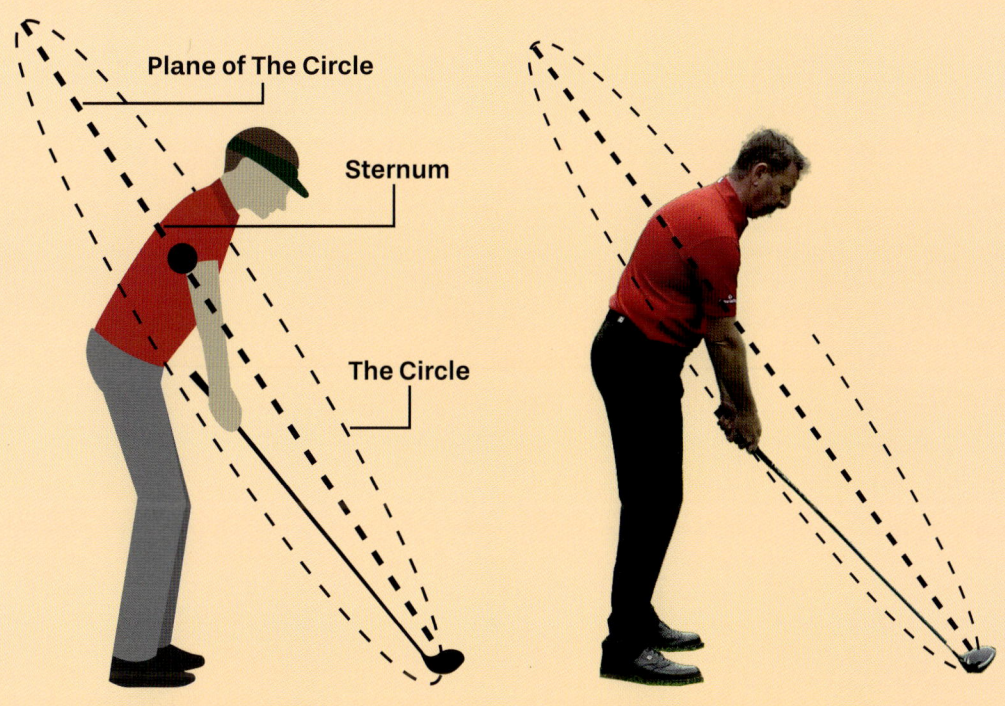

The clubhead moves on The Circle, which is angled on a line from the middle of the clubface to your sternum

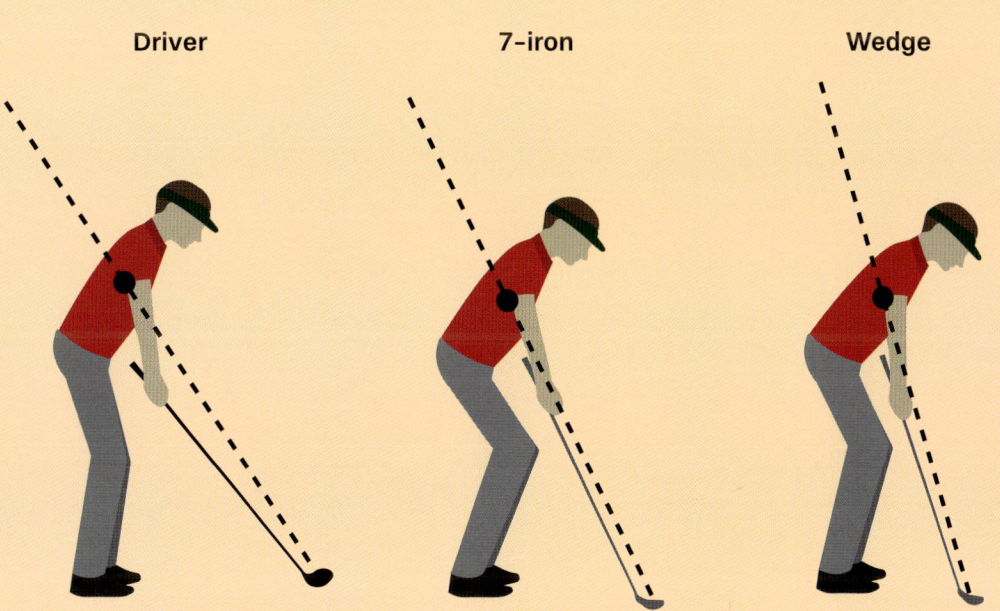

The angle of The Circle for different clubs

Rotate your body by pushing against the ground

How To Practise Turning Your Body

Begin with your body upright. You can either hold a stick (or club) across your chest or fold your arms. Look straight ahead at a distant object.

- Turn right by pushing on the ground to twist your hips and shoulders. Your eyes are still on the distant object
- Your front heel should come off the ground slightly and 75% of your weight should be on your back foot

Then use the ground to rotate the other way, with most of your back foot coming off the ground. As you come back to square, begin to look at a distant target, turning your head which allows your body to turn naturally to a full finish.

The sole of your back shoe faces away from the target. You are in balance with 100% of your weight on your front foot.

A common mistake is to slide the hips sideways. No, **rotate** the hips.

Repeat this flat swing lots of times. Turn right slowly to 'wind the spring'. Turn left faster to release it.

Turning Your Body For Real

Take a 7 iron and address a ball. Your spine angle changes from the vertical to a more forward posture. Think about the angle of The Circle which the clubhead is going to move round (from clubhead to sternum). Now use the ground as described above to rotate your body about your spine and move the club around The Circle. This turning of the body begins the backswing and creates power and speed.

What about the arms? Initially they do nothing, they are relaxed and simply transfer the power from the turning body to the clubhead. Towards the top allow your arms to rise a little.

And your eyes? Look at the ball during the backswing because this will help prevent you turning your head away from the ball.

THE GOLF SWING 23

WEIGHT TRANSFER

The transfer of weight through impact greatly increases the power, accuracy and consistency of your shots.

During the backswing shift 75% of your weight onto your back leg. Your eyes should remain on the ball. Your arms are relaxed (they don't need to be straight).

Initiate the downswing with your arms (NOT with your shoulders or you'll come 'over the top'). It feels like you're letting your arms drop. Then push with your back foot to turn your body round.

As your body rotates shift your weight onto your front leg.

You will initially be looking at the stationary ball then, just before contact, allow your eyes to follow the flight of the ball. If your head doesn't turn your body can't complete the turn.

You should finish with your chest facing the target and all your weight on your front foot. Hold the finish and lift your back foot off the ground to check the weight transfer.

The sequence is:

DOWN → **AROUND** → **THROUGH**

It's important to follow through fully. If you stop just after impact the clubhead will overtake your body, causing the ball to go left (or even slice to the right).

Practise rotating your body with a club, paying specific attention to the weight transfer

VIDEOS

To see a video of Julian demonstrating **practising the body turn**, please scan the QR code

COORDINATION OF BODY, ARMS & WRISTS

First let's practise cocking and releasing (uncocking) the wrists.

Take your grip on a club and set up as normal, but with the clubhead off the ground. Now cock your wrists so the **back** of the club moves round The Circle to make a short backswing. Then release your wrists so the **face** of the club moves back round The Circle to make a short downswing. This is the wrist action you want.

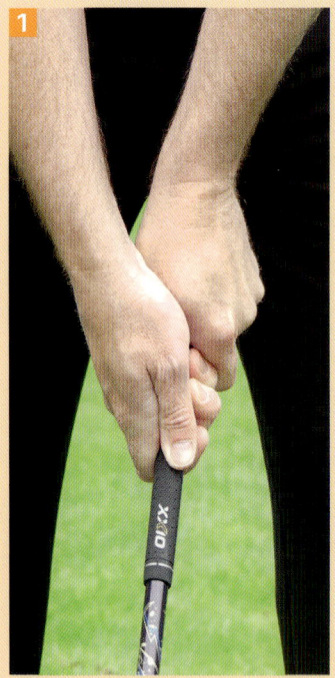
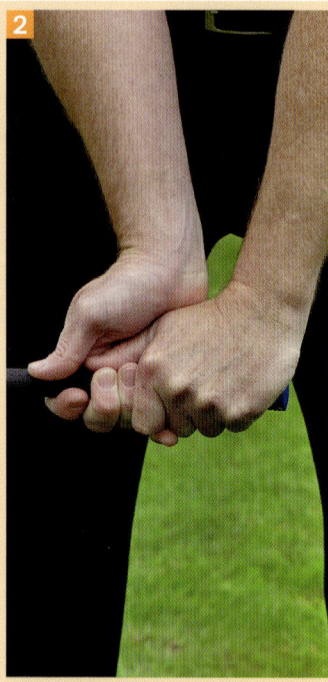
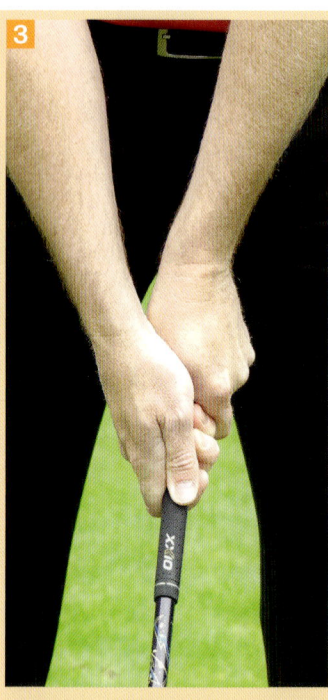

1. To practise cocking and releasing, start in the set-up position

2. Cock your wrists to take the club shaft horizontal

3. Then release them to take the club shaft down

VIDEOS

To see a video of Julian demonstrating **coordination in the golf swing**, please scan the QR code

Now for a **real swing**. The best way to improve coordination of body and wrists is to begin hitting balls with a half swing, then move on to a three-quarter swing and finally a full swing. Your objective is to have the maximum club speed just after impact with the ball, with the speed generated by body turn and wrist action. Resist the temptation to hit the ball with your arms.

Each time you swing check the angle of The Circle before you begin (it's roughly at a 45-degree angle).

For the **half swing** turn your body until the club shaft is horizontal, then turn back. Your body does all the work.

THE GOLF SWING 25

Half Swing

1. For the half swing, set up as normal

2. Turn your body right so the shaft is horizontal

3. Turn your body back and strike the ball

4. Follow through with the body and club

For the **three-quarter swing** turn the club round The Circle, gradually cocking your wrists so the back of the club is 'resting' on The Circle at the top of the backswing. Then make your downswing, releasing your wrists to make a swish as you progress. It's important to follow through, finishing with the face of the club 'resting' on The Circle.

Three-Quarter Swing

1. For the three-quarter swing, set up as normal

2. Turn your body until the shaft is horizontal

3. Continue the swing, cocking your wrists so the back of the club is 'resting' on The Circle

4. Make your downswing, releasing your wrists

5. Strike the ball

6. Follow through

7. Turn to face the target

8. Finish with the face of the club 'resting' on The Circle

THE GOLF SWING

For the **full swing** cock your wrists as above and allow them to stay cocked until you're well into the downswing. If you release too early you'll waste the power, too late and you'll slice the ball. Practice will make the precise timing come naturally. At the end of the swing make sure your chest is pointing at the target and the club shaft is touching your front shoulder.

1. For the full swing, set up as normal

2. Turn your body until the shaft is horizontal

3. Continue the swing, cocking your wrists

4. Complete the backswing

5. Start the downswing, keeping your wrists cocked

6. Release them in the final part of the downswing

7. Follow through with the club and body

8. Take the club past vertical ...

9. ... until it is resting on your shoulder

VIDEOS

To see a video of Julian demonstrating the **half, three-quarters and full swing,** please click on the QR code

RHYTHM

You need maximum clubhead speed just after you hit the ball. That way the club is still accelerating when it hits.

So there is no need for speed in the backswing. And the start of the downswing can be smooth too – accelerate from hip height all the way to the finish.

Listen to your swing: it should start to swish when the club nears the golf ball.

Rhythm is aided by swinging tension free.

BALANCE

If a car wheel is out of balance the steering wheel will wobble. In the same way if you are out of balance your swing will wobble. Not a good look!

If you can hold your finish until the ball lands, you're probably in balance. Even if it's a bad shot, hold the finish for six seconds (which is about the time of the flight of the ball) because some learning will take place while you're waiting for it to land.

REDUCING TENSION

Tension is the number one enemy of the golf swing. Muscles aren't designed to be locked, so do everything in a relaxed way. The body can then move and gain more speed.

If you know you have tensed up, perhaps due to other competitors or hazards in front of you, take a few deep breaths, tighten your hold on the club and then relax the tension to create awareness. Then concentrate on swinging the club tension-free.

MYTHS

I think it's important to challenge a few of the common misconceptions in golf, such as:
- Keeping your head down
- Keeping your front arm straight
- Keeping your front foot pinned to the ground

Keeping Your Head Down & Your Eyes On The Ball

Keeping your head down prevents your body turning through impact and often causes shots to go left of your target.

As an experiment, make your normal set-up and, when you're ready to play, keeping your head down, close your eyes and hit the ball with them shut. Try this a few times without over-thinking it.

Now try with your eyes open but, just before you hit the ball, start to look towards the target. Repeat a few times.

Is it true that you must keep your head down and your eyes on the ball?

Keeping Your Front Arm Straight

Keeping your front arm straight creates more tension in your swing.

Again this is an experiment, not a recommendation for play!

Make your normal set-up and in the backswing deliberately bend your front arm. Take a few shots like this. The outcome may surprise you: it's common for golfers to see an improvement in their ball striking and have a feeling of an easier swing when they do this.

Keeping Your Front Foot Pinned To The Ground

Allowing your front heel to rise slightly will prevent injury.

Try the swinging leg exercise. Take a shot as normal but on the backswing let your front leg swing across in front of your back leg. At the top of the backswing replace your front leg roughly where it started and let your back leg swing across in front of your front leg while the club hits the ball. Repeat and pay attention to the weight shift you experience.

Can you hit the ball ok with so much movement? Does your front foot really need to be pinned to the ground?

THE GOLF SWING

VIDEOS

To see a video of Julian demonstrating the **swinging leg exercise**, please scan the QR code

USING A TOWEL TO PRACTISE

Find a towel, roll it up lengthways, then tape around it in several places to keep it rolled. It should be at least as long as the distance from the ground to your hip.

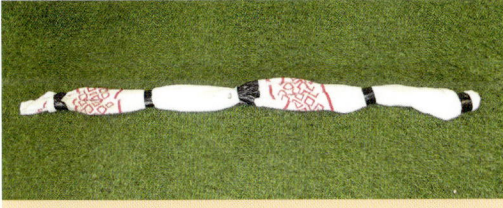

A towel ready for practice

You are now going to make continuous swings using the towel as a 'club'. Let's choose to imagine the towel is a **7 iron**:
- Find the point on the towel which gives the same length as a 7 iron's shaft
- Hold the towel there, in both hands, with your normal grip
- Relax
- Rotate your **body** to initiate the turn with the towel (don't cock your wrists yet)
- Go round The Circle cocking your wrists (and allowing your arms to rise a little as you turn)
- This will throw the towel over your back shoulder
- Change direction
- Allow your arms to fall
- Release your wrists to swish the towel through the bottom of the swing (where the ball would be)

Practise by making continuous swings with a towel

- Continue to turn your body towards the target and allow the towel to flow over your front shoulder
- Finish in balance with your chest facing the target
- Immediately begin the next swing so you are continuously swinging the towel, say ten times

Now move your hands on the towel so the bit you're swinging is shorter, like a **wedge**. Swing this 'towel wedge' ten times. The Circle is more upright, of course.

Next, move your hands to the end of the towel and swing this '**towel driver**' ten times. The Circle is flatter.

Repeat this exercise as often as possible at home. It helps your turning, weight transfer, rhythm, timing, coordination and balance.

You can also try swinging the towel with your eyes shut to heighten awareness of the movement and swing.

At last you're ready to take your towel to the driving range. Make five 'shots' with the towel the length of a 7 iron, then make five practice swings with a real 7 iron.

Try to swing the club with the same feeling as you had with the towel. Finally hit one shot with the 7 iron with that same feeling. Repeat this cycle several times.

Then try putting some speed into the bottom of the swings. You should be able to make both the towel and the club swish.

Try all of this with different clubs, adjusting the length of towel to suit each club's shaft length

Video yourself if you can. The aim is to make the real swing replicate the **feeling** of the towel swing. (**Feeling** is ten times more powerful than **thinking**.)

If you find yourself hitting the ball rather than swinging through it, put the ball on a short tee. This takes away part of the **hitting** instinct.

SUMMARY
The essentials are:

| TURN YOUR BODY | RELEASE YOUR WRISTS | TRANSFER YOUR WEIGHT |

When you practise, work on your body first, then your wrists.

Swing Thoughts
- Address the ball as in pages 16–19
- Imagine The Circle
- Imagine your arms are heavy. (This will stop you picking up the club as you begin the swing, and you can allow your arms to fall from the top of the backswing)
- Take a few relaxed, continuous practice swings
- Now swing the clubhead round The Circle, raising your front heel
- The back of the clubhead is now on The Circle
- Begin the downswing, keeping relaxed arms throughout
- Release your wrists to give a swish as you swing through the ball
- The **face** of the clubhead is now on The Circle
- Keep going to a relaxed finish: body facing the target; sole of back shoe facing away from the target; club shaft on your front shoulder

VIDEOS

To see a video of Julian demonstrating the **towel swing**, please scan the QR code

CHAPTER 3

WARMING UP & PRACTISING

In the first two chapters we have seen how to set up to the ball and how to swing a mid-range club like a 7 iron. In this chapter I'll show you how to warm up and then practise before a round.

WARMING UP

Ideally you need plenty of time to get your body ready to play. But sometimes this isn't possible, so I'll give both a short and a long routine.

Two-Minute Warm Up

Select three clubs of a similar length, e.g. your 6, 7 and 8 irons. Put two together side by side, then lay the third one on top of the other two. Grip the three handles with your hands apart.

Swinging smoothly and well within yourself:
- Make ten practice half swings with this heavy 'club'
- Then make ten three-quarter swings
- And finally ten full swings

Now discard one club. Take the same grip on the remaining two and make ten half swings, ten three-quarter swings and ten full swings.

Finally make the practice swings with just one club. The idea is to use the weight of the heavy clubs to get your body moving, then feel how much faster you can swing with a single club.

Hold the three clubs together

Longer Warm Up

Focus on the mobile joints you are going to use: ankles, hips, shoulders and neck.

1. Stand on one leg and rotate the other ankle in all directions. Now stand on the other leg and rotate the other ankle in all directions.

2. Stand and twist your hips. Then lie down on your back with your knees bent and swing your knees from side to side.

3. Hold the head of your driver in your left hand and the end of its shaft in your right hand. Now 'paddle' as if you were paddling a kayak.

Stand on one leg and rotate the other ankle in all directions

Lie on your back and swing your knees from side to side

'Paddle' while holding the driver at each end

4. Keeping the same grip or with each hand at the end of the club, twist your body so the clubhead moves to the left. Then twist the other way.

5. Finally, move your chin down and into your neck (giving you a double chin!) and rotate your shoulders up, back and down several times.

Once you're warmed up you're ready to hit some practice shots using a good pre-shot routine (which is detailed opposite) for each of a variety of clubs.

Twist your body while holding the driver at each end

With your chin compressed into your neck, rotate your shoulders up, back and down

VIDEOS

To see videos of Julian demonstrating the **two-minute warm up and the longer warm up**, please scan the QR code

THE BEST PRE-SHOT ROUTINE

Developing a pre-shot routine not only helps you prepare for each shot but also brings a sense of structure and confidence to your game.

1	Visualise	Take a moment to visualise the shot you want to hit. Picture the ball flight trajectory and landing spot. This mental image helps you focus on the desired outcome and builds confidence.
2	Select a target	Identify a specific target in the distance. It could be a spot on the fairway, a tree or any distinguishable point. This target serves as a reference point for alignment and helps you aim accurately.
3	Assess the conditions	Consider external factors such as wind speed and direction.
4	Take practice swings	Take a couple of practice swings to loosen up your muscles and get a feel for the swing. Focus on rhythm, tempo and balance. Listen to the club swishing – relax the arms and shoulders to make it louder.
5	Align your body	Position yourself parallel to the target line. Align your feet, hips and shoulders parallel to the target. Use an intermediate target on the ground, such as a divot or a blade of grass, to ensure accurate alignment.
6	Final check	Take a moment to review your grip, posture and ball position. Ensure that everything feels comfortable and is aligned correctly.
7	Breathe & relax	Take a deep breath to centre yourself and release any tension or nerves. Relax your mind and body, allowing you to enter a focused and calm state.
8	Commit	Once you are set up and ready to hit the shot make a commitment to your chosen target and swing. Trust your skills and the process you have gone through in your pre-shot routine.

VIDEOS

To see a video of Julian demonstrating the **pre-shot routine**, please scan the QR code

PRE-ROUND PRACTICE
Use your pre-shot routine to hit several balls with each of the following clubs (full swing unless specified):
- Wedge half swing
- Wedge three-quarter swing
- Wedge full swing
- 8 iron
- 6 iron
- Hybrid
- Fairway wood
- Driver

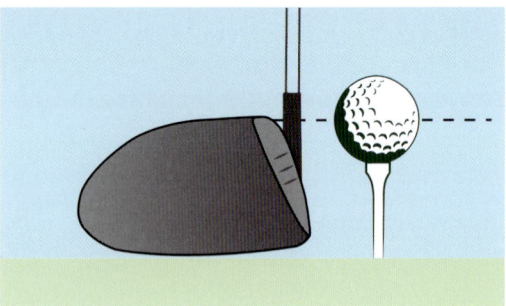

With the correct tee height, half the ball is above the driver's face

The last shot you make should be the one you plan to use from the first tee.

You will also need to do some putting practice. More on this later.

In your pre-shot practice, and on the course, your technique will vary slightly from club to club. This is discussed next. In later chapters we'll look at different kinds of shot: the chip, pitch, lob, bunker play, putting and so on.

THE DRIVER
1. Tee Height & Type Of Ball
The optimum tee height is when you can see half of the golf ball above the top of your driver.

I like the idea of using set-height tees as this takes out the guesswork. The height of your driver head will determine the length of tee you need.

Ideally get a friend to hold the driver next to the ball and tee so you can check that you can see half the ball.

If the tee is too high you will go underneath the ball and if it's too low you will hit low on the clubface and probably not get the ball in the air.

If you have a slow clubhead speed choose a softer ball, which will compress then spring forward. A slowly moving clubhead won't compress a hard ball – leave that to the pros!

2. Ball Position
The ideal ball position is opposite your left heel. The easiest way to check this is to put an alignment rod next to the ball pointing towards your body.

Check the position of the ball (opposite your front heel) with an alignment rod

The driver moves in a circle. The bottom of The Circle is in the centre of your stance, but you want to hit the ball as The Circle is starting to rise. That's why you have the ball forward in your stance.

3. Width Of Stance

The normal stance is a natural stride, but increase that by a shoe width for driving because you swing the driver fast and need stability for that.

Your normal stance is a natural stride, but increase that by a shoe width for driving

With the ball forward in your stance, the shaft of the driver should lean slightly backwards

Incorrect: if the shaft leans forwards you will be taking loft off the clubface and may be opening it

4. Weight Distribution

Normally you will have your weight 50-50 on each foot but with the driver it's better to make it 60-40 favouring your back foot. When you get it right it feels like you're pointing slightly upwards. The worst thing you can do with the driver is have too much weight on your front foot at address.

5. Posture

Take your stance as described in pages 16-19. Because the ball is forward in your stance the shaft of the driver will have a slight lean backwards. (If it's forwards you will be taking loft off the clubface and may be opening it.) Check that your weight is evenly distributed between your toes and heels to give a very stable base.

6. Alignment

You have already learnt to align your club, and parallel to that your feet, knees, hips and shoulders. However, with the driver I don't mind your feet pointing slightly to the right as this allows a bit more hip turn and lets you hit the inside of the ball more easily. The worst thing is to point your feet left, as you are likely to hit the outside of the ball and either pull or slice your tee shot.

7. Shoulders

I like to see the left shoulder higher than the right. This is because your right hand is lower than your left hand on the grip and the ball is forward in your stance. It feels as if you are pointing slightly upwards.

The left shoulder should be slightly higher to tie in with the height of your hands

8. Tension

Now that you are set up correctly I want you to think about one last thing and that is tension. So often I see golfers take a sharp intake of breath just before they start the backswing. This causes the body to tighten and the muscles shorten and will make you lose distance. Instead take a deep breath, hold it for two seconds and then breathe out. Make your golf swing without breathing in again.

9. The Backswing

Turn your **body** to start the backswing. This creates a natural width to the swing and helps with timing and rhythm. Once the shaft is at hip height begin to use your wrists in a natural throwing action like casting a fishing line. This moves the back of the clubface onto The Circle. Keep your front arm relaxed as you turn your shoulders to 90 degrees and your hips to 45 degrees. Your left thumb will be underneath the club, supporting it.

10. The Downswing

The clue is in the title: your arms move down (and your weight shifts onto your lead foot) putting the club into a position where you can strike the inside of the ball. At the same time your body turns left bringing your shoulders back to the address position and your hips start to open.

11. Through-Swing

Remember: keeping your head down is really bad.

Just before impact allow your eyes to begin following the flight of the ball. This allows your head to turn which encourages your body to turn and your weight to transfer. Your arms feel long until hip height and from this point your arms will start to fold naturally, allowing the club to flow over your shoulder. Your weight will have fully transferred onto your front foot, and your head, shoulders, hips and back knee will be pointing towards the target. You should be able to maintain a balanced finish and hold it until the golf ball lands. Simple really!

VIDEOS

To see videos of Julian demonstrating the **driver set-up and swing**, please click on the QR code

WARMING UP & PRACTISING

Driver

1. Set up with a wide stance and the ball positioned forward

2. Turn your hips and shoulders together which starts moving the club correctly

3. Just after hip height start to cock your wrists so the butt of the club points towards the ball

4. Your body turns completely, weight on the back foot, wrists fully cocked and the club parallel to the ground

5. Start moving your weight back to your front foot, turn your body and move the club back around The Circle

6. Release the clubhead; your weight still transferring to the front foot and shoulders returning back to the set-up position

7. The clubhead is fully released; your hips carry on turning, your shoulders are square and your weight moves onto the front foot

8. Your body turns left, your eyes start following the ball, your weight is 80% on the front foot and the club released around The Circle

9. Your body faces the target, your weight is on the front foot, balanced, with the club over your shoulder

FAIRWAY WOODS

Fairway woods (3, 5, 7, 9) come with a variety of lofts. Although you usually want to gain distance, the 3 wood is the least forgiving and many golfers find it difficult to hit. Only use it if you have a lie that lets the bottom edge of the club get below the bottom of the ball, and when the lie of the grass is with the stroke.

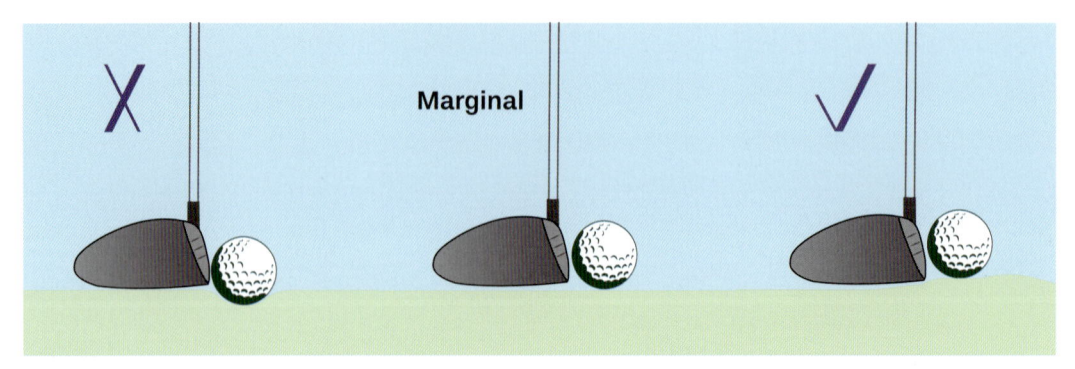

Only use a 3 wood if the bottom edge of the club can get below the ball

For any fairway wood the ball position is halfway forward in your stance. The stance is also slightly wider than normal. Otherwise the set-up and swing are as normal.

With a fairway wood, the stance is slightly wider than normal and the ball position is halfway forward in your stance

WARMING UP & PRACTISING

Fairway Wood

1. Set up with the ball just inside your front heel, your weight 60-40 towards the back foot and your body relaxed

2. Turn your hips and shoulders to move your arms and club away in one piece

3. Just after hip height cock your wrists, begin loading your weight onto your back foot and continue your shoulder turn

4. Your weight is 70-30 on the back foot, shoulders fully turned, club parallel to the ground, your front knee pointing behind the ball and front heel moving freely

5. Start the downswing by allowing your arms to move downwards, transferring your weight back towards your front foot

6. Your weight is moving onto your front foot, your body keeps turning and you fully release the clubhead

7. Your eyes should start to follow the ball enabling your head and body to turn and your weight to transfer

8. Your body continues to turn and your weight is 70-30 on the front foot, your wrists are re-cocking and back knee is pointing to the target

9. Your body faces the target, your weight is on the front foot, balanced with the club over your shoulders; hold for 6 seconds

HYBRID (RESCUE) CLUBS

If in doubt use a hybrid, they are brilliant! A hybrid is easier to hit than a long iron. They are versatile – use them from a poor lie, for chipping and anything up to a full shot. Hybrids come in a variety of lofts – I have two in my bag.

IRONS

Position the ball in the centre of your stance – this automatically gives a downward strike. The width of stance is your natural step, and the weight is 50–50 on each foot. The club shaft should have a slightly forward lean at address.

Weight transfer and releasing the clubhead are even more important than normal.

Hit through the shot, not down on it. You aren't trying to take a divot, but with the short irons and their more vertical swing it often happens. The key here is to hit the ball then the turf – you want the energy going into the ball not the ground.

With an iron, the stance is your natural stride and the ball position is in the centre of your stance

WARMING UP & PRACTISING   41

Iron

1. Set up with the ball central in your stance, your weight 50-50 and your body relaxed

2. Turn your body and shift your weight towards your back foot which moves the arms and club into position

3. Just after hip height cock your wrists, transferring your weight onto your back foot. Your arms can feel long but should be relaxed

4. Your body is fully turned, your weight is 80-20 on the back foot, the shaft parallel to the ground and your head turned slightly behind the ball

5. Your arms move down as you are transferring your weight back to your front foot; turn your body back towards the ball with a 90° angle between your arms and club

6. Start to release the clubhead when your hands reach hip height. Your weight is still moving back towards the ball

7. Fully release the clubhead at impact; your weight still moving towards the front foot and your arms back to the set-up position

8. Your head follows the ball, your body turns to the target; the back heel comes up, arms long and relaxed but not stretched forward

9. Finish your swing with your weight on the front foot, body facing the target, balanced and the club finishing over your shoulder

CHAPTER 4

THE CHIP, PITCH & LOB

In this chapter I'll talk about ways to get close to the flag from off the green. Here we'll look at the pitch, the chip and the lob, with putting covered later.

First some definitions:
- A **chip** is a shot that rolls more than it flies
- A **pitch** flies more than it rolls
- A **lob** goes high and stops quickly

In order of difficulty a putt is the easiest stroke, followed by a chip, then a pitch and finally a lob, which can be tricky.

For each of these strokes you're aiming to land on a predictable surface wherever possible. And that means you should try to land on the green rather than the fringe.

THE CHIP

Your objective is to land the ball just on the green, but with enough speed so it runs on to the hole. This way you have the shortest swing, which is more accurate.

The loft of the club creates more or less roll. Use a hybrid if you want a long roll then – for a gradually shorter roll – a 7 iron, an 8 iron, a pitching wedge or a sand wedge.

With a chip, aim to land just on the green

THE CHIP, PITCH & LOB   43

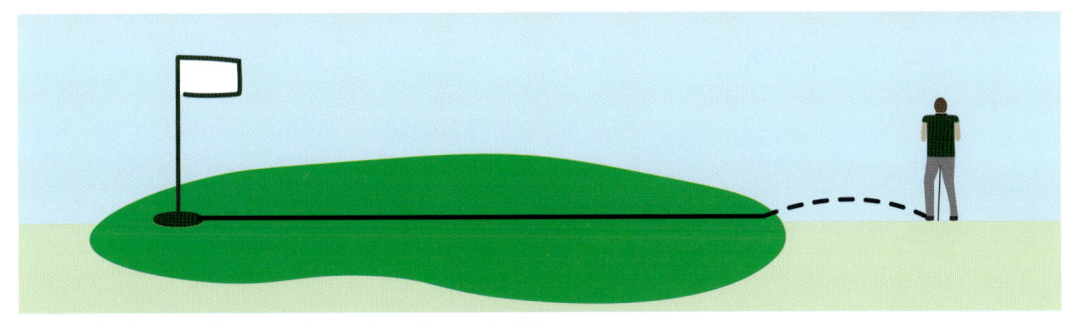

Use a hybrid or 7 or 8 iron to roll to a pin at the back of the green

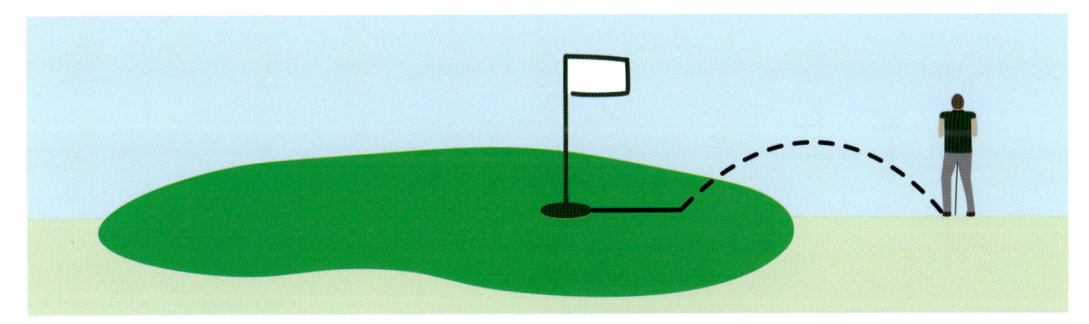

Use a pitching wedge or sand wedge if the pin is near the front of the green

Chipping Set-Up

Set up with a narrow stance, maybe a clubhead width between your feet. This will prevent over-hitting.

Stand much closer and much taller than usual, giving a more in-line swing path. It doesn't matter if the heel of the club is off the ground.

Put your weight 50-50 on both feet, or 60-40 favouring your front foot.

Your feet should be square to or fractionally left of the target to prevent too much sidespin.

It's ok to grip down the club and you can use your putting grip if you prefer. But make sure you have equal pressure on both hands and you're holding the club lightly.

For a chip, stand closer and taller than usual with a narrow stance

Chipping Technique

A chip should be like a putt: **don't move your wrists**. Poor chippers try to lift the ball, but rather let the loft of the club do that for you.

It's really important to select the right club (see above). If you're not sure of the geometry use 25% carry and 75% roll as a guide.

Swing the club at constant speed, i.e. with no acceleration. This is more predictable.

THE PROPER GOLFING HANDBOOK

The Chip

1. Set up with 1 clubhead's width between your feet, the ball in the centre, your feet closer to the ball and your body more upright

2. Start the backswing with your arms and club moving in one piece. The clubhead should stay close to the ground

3. Your hands move just past your back leg, with your arms and club remaining long and straight, your weight 50–50

4. Start the downswing aiming to return back to your set-up position with a bit of speed

5. The impact should look similar to set-up with the club striking the bottom of the ball and the club facing your target

6. With a gentle weight transfer forward, your arms and club remain long and close to the ground; keep the club speed constant

7. Your weight is moving forward, no wrist cocking, just focus on your arms staying long and the club being an extension of them

8. Gently turn towards the target as your weight keeps moving forward

9. The follow-through is similar length to the backswing; 70% of your weight is on the front foot; watch the flight of the ball

Chipping From A Downhill Slope
Choose a wedge or a sand wedge, to get some loft.
- Set up with your spine vertical. To do this you'll need to bend your back (uphill) knee
- During the swing, cock your wrists to lift the clubhead, or it will hit the slope. Release the wrists on the downswing
- Your weight will transfer onto your front foot. You should be aiming to stay in balance due to the nature of the shot
- The ball will fly lower and have more roll which you will need to allow for. These shots should be practised as much as possible

1. Set up with your front leg straight, back leg flexed and your spine upright. Adjust the stance width to the slope's severity

2. Start the backswing by cocking your wrists to avoid hitting the slope, with your weight even between your feet

3. At impact, your wrists are released to power the clubhead under the ball to give it loft, with your weight still centred

4. Finish the swing with your arms long, your head and body turning towards the target and remaining in balance

THE PROPER GOLFING HANDBOOK

Chipping From An Uphill Slope
Choose a pitching wedge.
- Set up with your spine vertical. You'll need to bend your front (uphill) knee
- On the downswing the clubhead will inevitably touch the ground. Don't worry about this restricting your follow-through, and expect to take a divot
- This shot flies higher than normal and stops quicker. You will need to allow for this

1. Set up with your front leg slightly bent, your back leg and spine straight. The stance is 2-3 clubheads' width, the ball central

2. Start the backswing with no additional wrist action, your weight staying 50-50 and your shoulders turning slightly

3. At impact return back to the set-up position but with momentum moving forwards, the club striking the bottom of the ball

4. Finish with your weight 60-40 to the front foot, body facing the target, arms comfortably long but starting to bend depending on the slope's severity

VIDEOS

To see videos of Julian demonstrating the **chip,** please scan the QR code

To see videos of Julian demonstrating **chipping from a downhill and uphill slope,** please scan the QR code

THE PITCH

Remember, a pitch flies more than it rolls. You typically use it when you're 20-80 yards (18-73m) from the pin. The idea is to get the ball to stop quicker than if you chipped.

Club selection is vital. There are four clubs you can use and I list them here in increasing order of loft (resulting in the ball going higher and higher):
- Pitching wedge, e.g. 40-45 degrees
- Gap wedge, e.g. 45-50 degrees
- Sand wedge, e.g. 54-56 degrees
- Lob wedge, e.g. 58-64 degrees

I don't recommend opening the clubface (pointing to the right of the target). Leave that for short lobs.

I do however recommend keeping the grooves in the clubface very clean. You need the grooves to help create backspin, which gives the ball loft.

Set-Up
- The width of your stance should be between two clubheads and your normal pace. This is different from chipping, where your feet are almost together
- Set your feet square to the target
- Set your clubface square to the target
- Have your weight 60% on your front foot

Making The Shot
You are **not** going to take the clubhead round The Circle and you are going to cock your wrists in a different way – to bring the shaft towards the vertical.

For a very short pitch of, say, 20 yards (18m) there is little arm movement:
- Turn the club through 90 degrees using just your wrists. The shaft is now horizontal to the right
- Now release your wrists so the club moves back to the ball and give a small follow-through until the shaft is horizontal to the left
- Make sure there is a gentle weight shift forward to guarantee a downward strike

Your pitching stance is wider than for chipping – between two clubheads and your normal stride

THE CHIP, PITCH & LOB

The Pitch

1. Set up with a narrow stance (c. 2 clubheads' width), the ball central; stand slightly closer to the ball than normal, stay relaxed

2. Start the backswing by cocking your wrists, your weight even between your feet and your shoulders turning to the right

3. At hip height there will be a 45° angle between your club and arm

4. The length of backswing will depend on the length of shot and the club used. Your weight should stay even on both feet

5. Start the downswing by moving your arms downwards, creating a natural 45° angle between your arms and club

6. Just before impact start to release the clubhead towards the ball; remember not to hold the clubface open

7. At impact you should be similar to set-up, but with your weight moving towards the front foot

8. Through impact keep your body turning towards the target and your weight moving forwards; the club is an extension of your arms

9. Finish with your weight on your front foot and body turned to the target; your arms long and relaxed, finishing about hip height

THE CHIP, PITCH & LOB

Longer Pitch

For a longer pitch you start to use your body as well:
- Turn your body to make a quarter turn
- Now cock your wrists so the club shaft is more vertical
- Release your wrists
- Turn through to face the target, with all your weight on your front foot
- The overall feeling is like a pendulum swinging back and then forward with a consistent speed and rhythm
- Try to keep the lengths of the backswing and through-swing equal

1. Set up with your feet 2 clubheads' width apart, weight 50-50 and the ball central; you can stand closer to the ball and be more upright

2. Start the backswing aiming to make a quarter turn and allow your wrists to become more active

3. At hip height there will be a 45° angle between your lead arm and club, your weight will be about 60-40 favouring your back foot

4. At the top of your backswing your wrists will have cocked upwards creating a 90° angle between your front arm and the club

5. To start the downswing allow your arms to move downwards as your body starts to turn back towards the ball

6. Just before impact start to release the clubhead, your weight moving back to 50-50 and your shoulders square

7. At impact you have fully released the clubhead under the ball, your weight is now 60-40 to your front foot

8. Keep your body turning through impact, your weight is now 70-30 to your front foot; the club feels like an extension of your arms

9. Finish facing the target, with a 90° angle between your arm and club, making sure you are in balance

Adjusting The Distance Still Further

You can make the ball go further still by making a half turn before cocking your wrists. And if you need even more distance you can of course make a standard 'Round The Circle' shot, cocking your wrists so that the back of the club is on The Circle at the top of the backswing, etc …

You can also try pitching with the other pitching clubs. Initially practise with a sand wedge and find how far the ball goes for the types of swings above. Repeat this for the other pitching clubs and record the distances to make a pitching chart. (You could use technology to measure the distances of your shots for more accurate feedback.)

Type of shot	Pitching distance (yards)
Wrists only	18
Quarter turn + wrists	30
Half turn + wrists	45
Full shot	70

Pitching chart for a pitching wedge

VIDEOS

To see a video of Julian demonstrating **pitching over different distances**, please scan the QR code

Pitching From A Difficult Lie

If there's not much grass under the ball, cock your wrists steeply to make sure that when you release on the downswing you come into the ball at a steep angle and hit the ball first, i.e. before the club hits the ground.

If you have a really difficult lie you can exaggerate this technique by having the ball further back in your stance and by leaning the club shaft forward at address. These adjustments reduce the bounce on the club which can then penetrate the ground better.

You can exaggerate this even more by closing the clubface a little.

Playing off this lie often results in a lower ball flight with more roll which you will need to allow for and should be practised.

Make a steep downswing when pitching from a difficult lie

THE CHIP, PITCH & LOB 51

Pitching From A Difficult Lie

1. Set up with a slight shaft lean forwards and the ball central

2. The shaft leaning slightly forwards makes it easier to cock your wrists at the start of the backswing

3. With your hands at hip height the clubhead should be higher than them; your weight similar to set-up, your shoulders rotating back

4. At the top of the backswing there should be a 90° angle between your arm and the club

5. Start the downswing by moving your arms downwards but maintain the wrist cock so the clubhead comes down steeply

6. Just before impact release the clubhead and maintain its speed so you can move the club down and under the ball

7. At impact fully release the club, your weight moving onto your front foot; keep the club accelerating

8. Keep your body and head turning towards the target, moving your weight onto the front foot

9. Finish with your weight on your front foot facing the target and the club re-cocking upwards

THE LOB

Make a lob shot when you need the ball to go high and stop when it lands. Really the higher the ball goes the better!

(Note that a lob and a bunker shot are very similar.)

You need a good lie to get the club under the ball.

Since you need a lot of loft, use a sand wedge or a lob wedge. If you need even more loft use one of these and open the clubface as follows:

- Twist the club shaft to open the clubface
- Then take your grip
- Gradually open your stance until the club's leading edge is at right angles to the target

- There should be only two clubheads' width between your feet
- The ball is in the middle of your (new) stance
- The club handle is in the middle of your body
- Make a steep backswing
- Make the downswing **in line with your feet.** You are cutting under the ball
- Complete your follow-through to give some power. Otherwise, with so much loft, the ball won't go far enough

Note that the ball spins right but your leftward stance compensates for this, giving a straight shot.

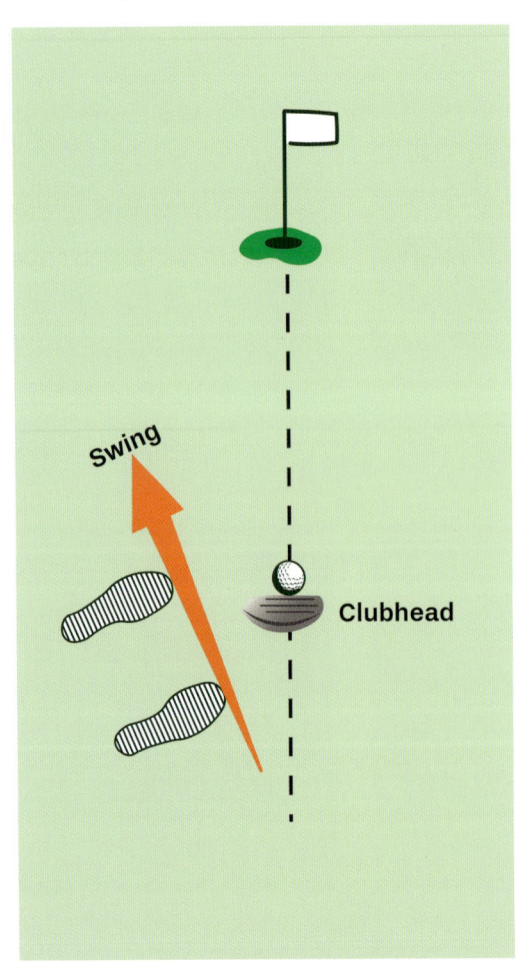

Set-up for a lob: Your feet are open and the swing is in line with them, but the clubface points towards the target

THE CHIP, PITCH & LOB 53

The Lob

1. Set up with an open stance, use a lob wedge or open the face of your sand wedge with the ball in the centre of your stance

2. Begin the backswing with an early wrist cock to help with a more upright backswing

3. Turn the hips and shoulders as you swing the club in an upright direction

4. At the top of your backswing there should be a full wrist cock so the club goes past vertical

5. Start the downswing by allowing your arms to move downwards and a gentle weight transfer forward

6. Release your wrists so that you can present the correct loft of the club to the ball

7. At impact fully release your club under the ball so you get the height on the shot, keeping the club accelerating

8. Keep your body turning towards the target and transfer your weight forwards

9. Finish with the club over your shoulder, your weight forwards and body facing the target in balance

VIDEOS

To see videos of Julian demonstrating the **lob shot** and the **lob shot from the rough**, please scan the QR code

A Lob From Deep Grass

Use a club with lots of loft, e.g. a sand wedge.

You can't go through the grass so you have to come down into it. Try to swing more vertically rather than around.

Cock your wrists on the backswing to bring the club shaft vertical, then release them on the downswing. Use gravity to bring the club down. (What goes up must come down!)

Follow through to a full finish.

1. Set up with the ball central, weight even or slightly forwards; use a lob wedge or open the face of your sand wedge

2. Start the backswing with an early wrist cock which moves the club upwards very quickly making the shot much easier

3. With your hands around hip height the wrists should be fully cocked and your weight even between your feet

4. At the top of the backswing your hips and shoulders should have turned, with the angle of the club feeling nice and upright

5. Start the downswing aiming to move the club down nice and steep while your body starts to turn back towards the ball

6. Just before impact release your wrists so you can move the loft of the club under the ball

7. At impact you are in a similar position as set-up but with momentum moving forwards

8. Through impact keep the clubhead accelerating and your weight moving forwards; use speed to get the ball out of the deep grass

9. Complete your finish with your weight forward, your body facing the target and the club over your shoulder

CHAPTER 5

BUNKER SHOTS

Next we need to know how to get out of the sand.

Luckily a bunker shot is very similar to a lob, which we covered in the last chapter. You also have a club specifically designed to help you, i.e. a sand wedge. What could possibly go wrong?

Getting out of the middle of a bunker is covered first, then I'll look at the trickier cases of clearing from the front and back of a bunker and dealing with a ball buried deep in the sand.

The Sand Wedge
The sand wedge has a curved bottom edge called a **Bounce**. This prevents the club digging into the sand too far. What happens is that the club rides through the sand and under the ball which is lifted out on a cushion of sand. It's the only shot where the club makes no contact with the ball!

The Set-Up
Align your feet parallel to the target, shoulder-width apart. Float the clubface above the sand and square to the target. There is no need to open your stance or the clubface.

The low point of your swing should be just behind the ball so set up with the ball one ball-width in front of the middle of your stance.

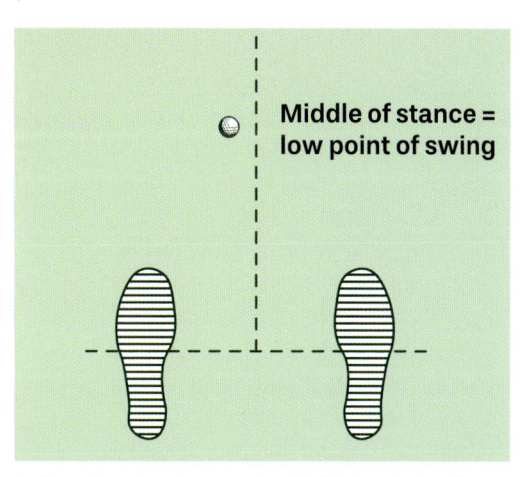

The Bounce

Ball position for a bunker shot (right-handed golfer)

THE PROPER GOLFING HANDBOOK

Feet parallel to the target with the ball one ball-width in front of the middle of your stance

Making The Stroke

Remember: What goes up must come down! Begin the backswing as normal but almost immediately cock your wrists so the club shaft is more vertical. The backswing is very **upright** – don't swing **around**.

Make a firm downswing and follow through to a full finish. You need lots of speed to make the clubhead go through the sand. It should feel like the momentum is being kept all the way through.

The distance the ball flies is controlled by the speed of your swing, but whatever speed you choose do complete the swing.

VIDEOS

To see a video of Julian demonstrating the **bunker shot**, please scan the QR code

1. For the bunker shot, set up with the ball just in front of central, shaft straight, club facing your target, weight even and feet dug in

4. At the top of the backswing the club goes over your back shoulder and your weight still feels centred

7. At impact, your club strikes the sand just before the ball, your wrists are fully released and your weight is moving onto your front foot

BUNKER SHOTS 57

2. Start the backswing by cocking your wrists upwards and turning your hips and shoulders; don't put too much weight on your back foot

3. Make sure you have fully cocked your wrists upwards, your lead arm can be long but must feel relaxed

5. Start the downswing by bringing the club down at a steep angle with your shoulders and hips turning back towards the ball

6. Just before impact release your wrists, bringing the club down at a steep angle to get the clubhead under the ball

8. Through impact your weight moves forward, the clubhead has moved some sand under the ball and is starting to swing upwards

9. At the finish you are facing the target, weight on your front foot, club over your shoulder and in balance

Ball At The Front Of The Bunker
Stand with your spine vertical – you may need to bend your front leg to achieve this. Dig your feet in for stability. Swing as described previously and finish the shot, though the follow-through may be restricted by hitting the sand or lip of the bunker.

Ball At The Back Of The Bunker
Sometimes the ball is so close to the back of the bunker that you can't make a swing (position A in the diagram). One solution is to chip out sideways to position B. Make sure that you chip far enough so that the next shot is **not** over the bunker – or the ball may go in again!

Occasionally there will be a flat bit at the edge of the bunker and you may be able to run the ball out sideways over it.

At the front of the bunker, stand with your spine vertical, possibly with your front leg bent

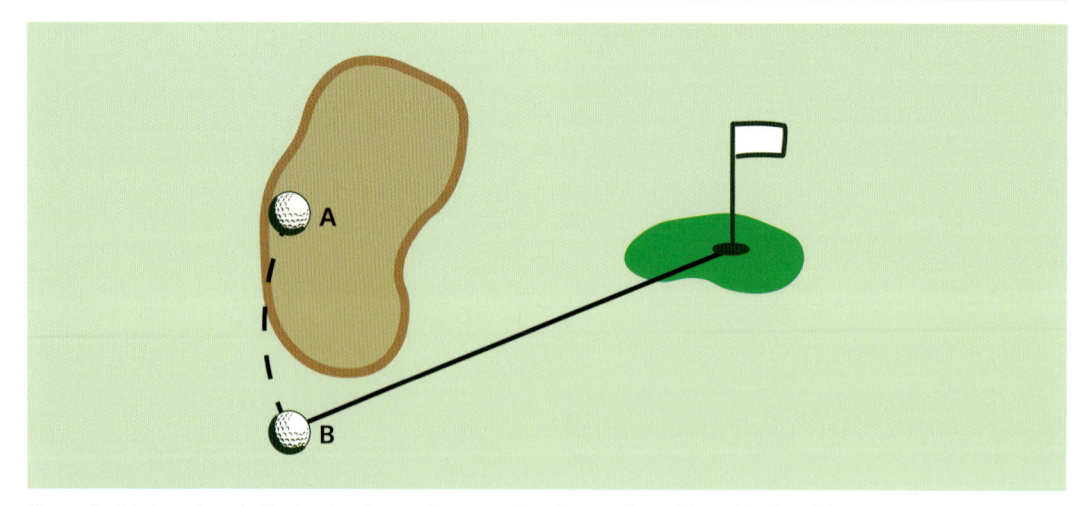

If your ball is too close to the back edge and you can't make a swing, chip out to the side

Ball Buried Deep In The Sand
Close the clubface at address. This reduces the Bounce which is helpful because this time you **want** the club to dig in. Repeat the swing as described above and remember to accelerate the club. Don't quit on the shot.

VIDEOS
To see a video of Julian demonstrating the **bunker shot with the ball buried deep**, please scan the QR code

BUNKER SHOTS

1. If the ball is buried deep in the sand, set up with your clubface slightly closed, the ball just forward of centre, and your weight 50-50

2. Start the backswing with an early wrist cock moving the club upwards, and a slight weight transfer onto your back foot

3. When your hands have reached hip height your club should be feeling very upright

4. Complete your backswing with a full wrist cock and 60-40 weight transfer onto your back foot

5. To start the downswing swing the club down steeply, move your weight back to 50-50 as your hips and shoulders turn back

6. Just before impact release the clubhead back to its set-up position, and move your weight forwards

7. At impact accelerate the club into the sand and under the ball; the clubface points towards the target

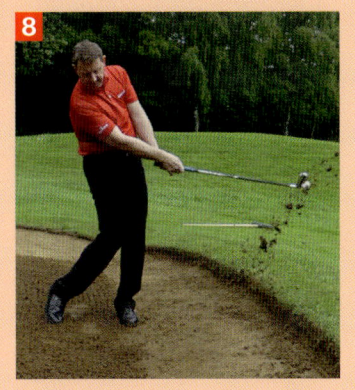

8. Turn your hips and shoulders towards the target, keep the clubhead accelerating. Note the position of the back knee

9. Finish with the club over your shoulder, weight on your front foot and your body facing the target

High & Short Bunker Shot

This is a shot that requires practice. Choose a lofted club if you have one, e.g. a lob wedge.

You may need to open up the face to add even more loft if the shot requires it. Sometimes you'll need to align your feet and body more to the left to compensate for the open clubface.

When swinging the club, maintain an upright backswing and follow the body line with the swing path. Try to maintain the loft of the club through impact and keep the speed constant. Any deceleration will probably result in the ball staying in the bunker as it won't have enough speed to carry any distance.

If you need to open up the clubface to add even more loft, align your feet and body more to the left to compensate

High & Short Bunker Shot

1. Open stance and open clubface; your body points left of the target so the clubface points towards it; normal stance width and the ball slightly forward of centre

2. Start the backswing with an early wrist cock upwards, following the line of your body alignment

3. When your hands have reached hip height your club should feel very upright with a shoulder and hip turn

4. At the top of your backswing your wrists are fully cocked, your weight 60-40 favouring the back foot

5. Bring the club down steeply, your shoulders and hips turning back towards the ball and weight moving back to 50-50

6. Just before impact release your wrists to return the clubhead back to its original position

7. Accelerate the open clubface under the ball; your weight moves forwards and your hips and shoulders return to the set-up position

8. Through impact your weight is 70-30 forwards, your hips and shoulders turning towards the target and club accelerating to get height

9. Finish facing the target with your weight on your front foot and the club over your shoulder

As with all shots in golf the bunker shots need practice. Golfers often shy away from this but practising is essential if you want to become proficient.

CHAPTER 6

PUTTING

Putting is a game within a game. No physical effort is needed so in theory anyone, from a young child to a pensioner, should be able to putt well. Almost 40% of your strokes are putts, so they make a big difference to your score. Read on for some key tips.

The Putting Grip

There are many ways to hold the putter, and they are all good. Experiment until you find the best grip for you. Also try different thicknesses of grip.

You can get a feel for the grip by abandoning the putter, then pushing your palms together. Note the equal pressure on each. This is your aim when you're putting for real. With equal pressure the face of the putter is stable so won't twist. But if the right hand takes over then the ball will go left, and vice-versa. It's important not to hold the club too tightly or the swing will be restricted. Remember '**Light not Tight**', particularly for long putts.

VIDEOS

To see a video of Julian demonstrating **putting grips**, please scan the QR code

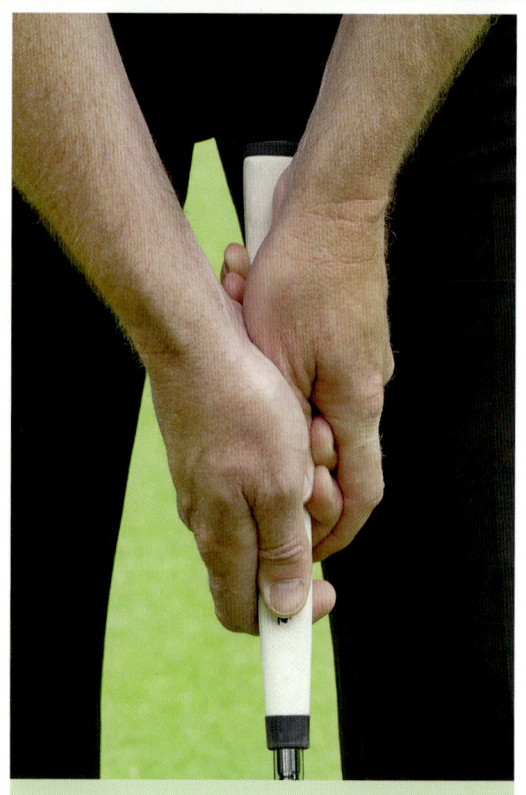

Hold the putter with a light grip, with equal pressure from both hands

PUTTING

Setting Up & Making The Stroke
- Grip the club, then stand upright with your arms hanging at full length
- Move forward towards the ball until the club shaft is almost vertical. It's always a mistake to stand too far from the ball
- The ball should be central in your stance, or slightly forward of that

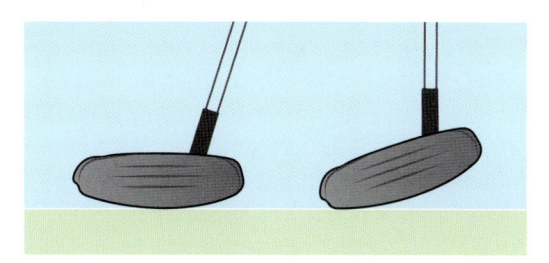

The bottom of this putter is rounded. So, with the shaft vertical, the club is still flat where it touches the ground

Speed & Line
Both the speed and the line of the putt are vital, but which is more important?

The answer is speed. If the speed is correct the ball won't finish up too far from the hole, leaving a simple putt in.

Speed
The optimum speed will take the ball one foot past the hole. (Note that if the speed were to take the ball two feet past the hole you have effectively shrunk the hole by 50% – see the diagram below.)

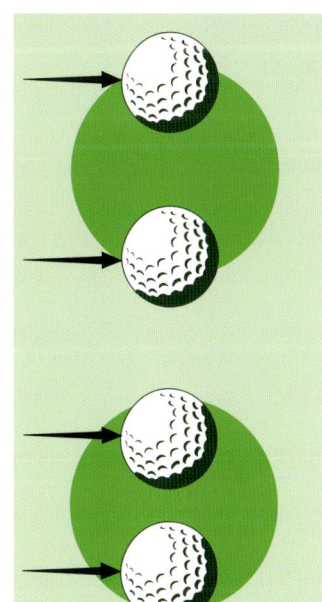

Stand with the club shaft almost vertical and the ball central to your stance, or slightly forward

If these golf balls are going slowly then gravity will pull them into the hole; if they're going too fast they will shoot over

At faster speed these balls would probably drop in – they need to be much nearer the centre of the hole

This set-up will allow you to swing on a straighter swing path. (Note that the bottom of the putter is rounded so it doesn't matter if the heel is off the ground, the rest of the club is still flat where it touches the ground.)

The overall effect of speed is like shrinking the size of the hole by 50%

Try to keep the backswing and through-swing equal in length and at a constant speed. (If a putt requires a 10mph swing you don't want to go from 8mph to 12mph hoping that you hit it at 10mph!)

On the practice green practise by putting to the fringe of the green, not to a hole. That way you can concentrate on speed. Also you can't miss, which is good for your confidence. Putt to different fringe distances to increase your speed control further.

When you have speed licked, practise putting to some holes with one ball – each time putting out (continuing to putt till the ball is in the hole).

You might also like to try putting with your eyes closed to get more feel, heighten awareness and gain feedback. I think you will be surprised at the result. If nothing else your stroke will become smoother. (Note you can practise chipping with your eyes closed too!)

Line

Few greens are flat. Any curve in the surface will make the ball roll offline – this is **the break**.

Look at the green as you approach it, to get clues about the break. In the diagram below there is raised ground to the far left of the green and a bunker to the near right. So you will expect the green to slope from the far left to the near right.

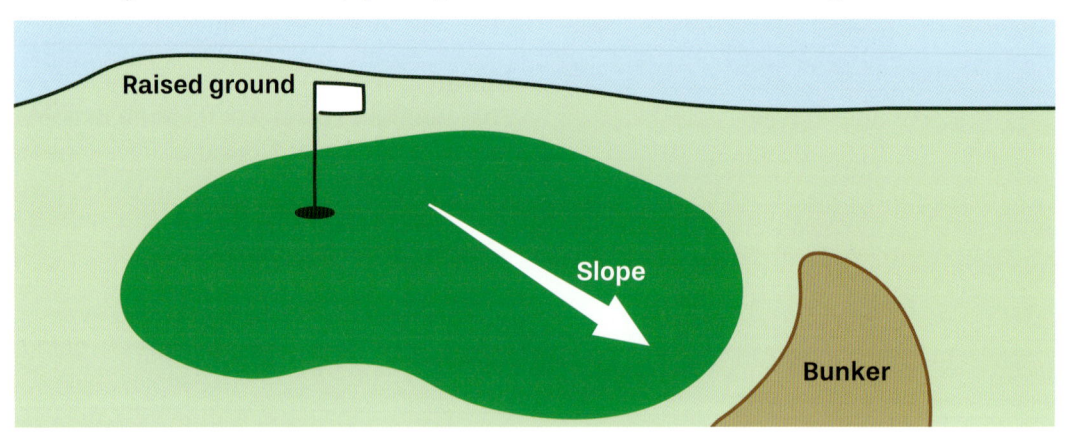

The slope will usually be from the higher ground to the lower ground

Once on the green, view the break from **behind the hole**. This is the only view I trust!

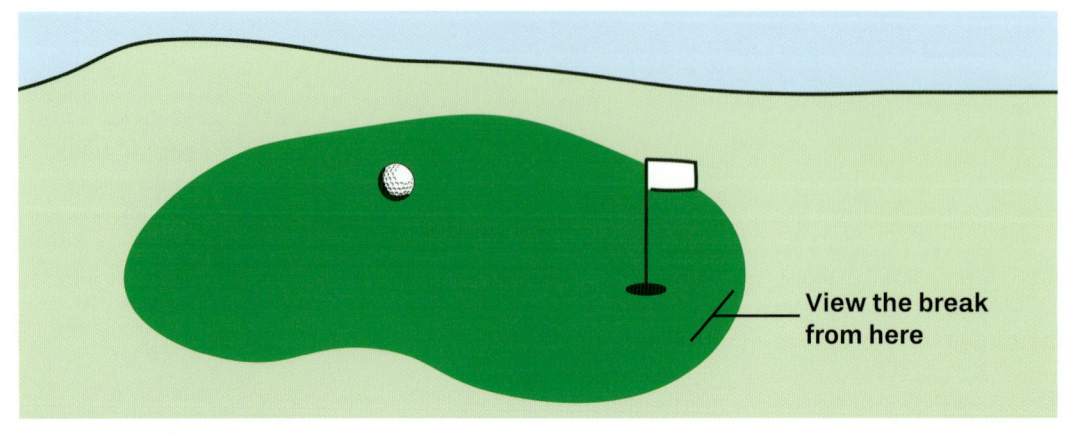

View the break from behind the hole

PUTTING 65

Also, if you have time, stand halfway from the ball to the hole straddling the line. The difference in pressure on your feet will give another clue about the break.

If your playing partner is putting first, watch their shot carefully to see the break in action. (Note that the rules don't allow you to stand directly behind them **while they are hitting the ball**. So stand behind them and to one side.)

When you're about to make a breaking shot, visualise the curving path. Aim at the 'top' of the curve, and leave gravity to do the rest.

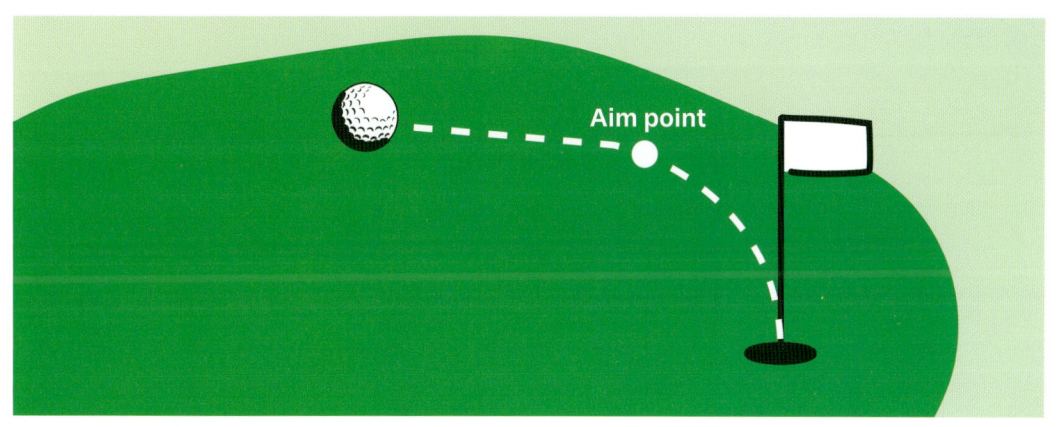

Aim at the top of the curve

Making Your Stroke

- Assess the speed and line as described above
- If you're more than eight feet (2.4m) from the hole calm your mind by telling yourself that you're not really expected to sink the putt. So relax! As close to the hole as possible is good enough
- Make practice strokes looking at the target, to get a feel for speed
- Swing back and forward the same distance
- The strokes should be smooth and at constant speed. (For chipping and putting you don't accelerate the clubhead)
- Now for the shot. Focus on the ball. Really look at it – notice the dimples, the shape of the back of the ball, anything that interests you about it
- Make the shot looking at the ball, and thinking of nothing else
- Only look at the hole after you've hit the ball. And enjoy the sound of it going in …

VIDEOS

To see a video of Julian demonstrating **putting**, please scan the QR code

THE PROPER GOLFING HANDBOOK

The Putt

1. Start with an upright set-up position, standing closer to the ball with the ball in the centre (or just forward) and a light, even grip

2. Move your shoulders, arms and club together; there will be a slight arc inwards as you're standing a distance from the ball

3. Keep the putter low to the ground and your weight even between your feet to stabilise the stroke

4. The length of backswing should vary depending on the length of the putt

5. Start the downswing, swinging the putter at a constant speed rather than trying to accelerate

6. Just before impact your putter should be swinging smoothly with the grip pressure still even

7. At impact you look similar to when you set up, with your clubface returning back to square

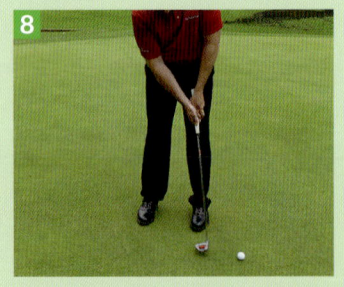

8. The putter moves forwards on an arc with the clubface pointing slightly left of target; keep an even grip pressure and your head still

9. Holding your finish until you hear the ball drop is a good habit to adopt but not essential

SUMMARY OF THE WRIST MOVEMENT IN THE SHORT GAME
(Last Three Chapters)

- For a standard shot go round The Circle, cocking your wrists so that the back of the club lies on The Circle in the backswing
- When putting try to get the shaft vertical, and don't use your wrists
- A chip is like a putt, no wrist movement
- For a pitch and a lob make a quarter turn, then use your wrists to bring the club shaft vertical

CHAPTER 7

SHOT SHAPING

We have been through how to make all the shots. Now we turn to the subject of getting them to go in the direction you want.

Although most golfers struggle to send the ball straight, there are times when it's useful to be able to bend the ball. You might use this:
- To get the ball around an obstacle such as a very tall tree
- To gain distance – a draw goes further (and a fade goes less far)
- To get to the pin. For example, if there is a bunker to the front and right of the green you may want to come in from the left (see diagram)
- To take advantage of weather conditions. For example, with a wind blowing from right to left aim right and draw the ball so it's flying downwind

A Touch Of Theory

The ball's flight is influenced by three things: the clubface, the swing path, the angle of attack (how steeply the club descends onto the ball). To keep things simple, we'll ignore the angle of attack for the time being.

In the following sections on how to bend

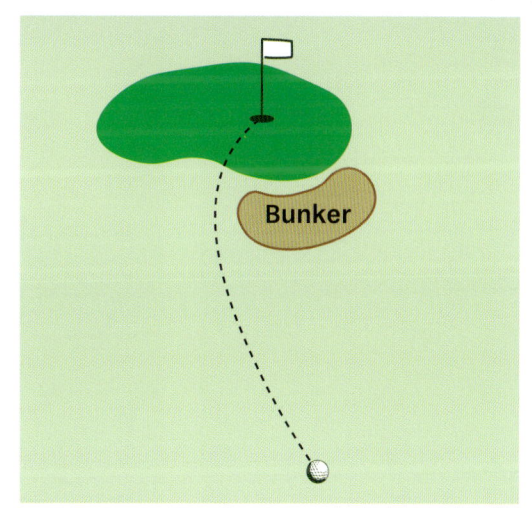

Fade your approach shot so it avoids the bunker, even if it's short

the ball remember:
- The clubface **sends** the ball in the initial direction
- The swing path **bends** the ball's flight

In short: the clubface sends, the swing bends.

HOW TO FADE THE BALL

In a fade the ball bends to the right. A fade is easier than a draw for high handicappers because of their poor movement – and they often slice rather than draw!

The diagram shows a typical situation where you've decided to fade the ball around a huge, high tree:

1. Set the clubface first to start the ball towards the left of the tree
2. Then set your foot and body lines a bit further left
3. Then swing along the foot line
4. During the swing do **not** release your wrists through impact. The idea is to maintain the clubface position you set at address throughout the swing and particularly at impact

It's a bit like a slice spin in tennis: you swing across the ball and it bends right.

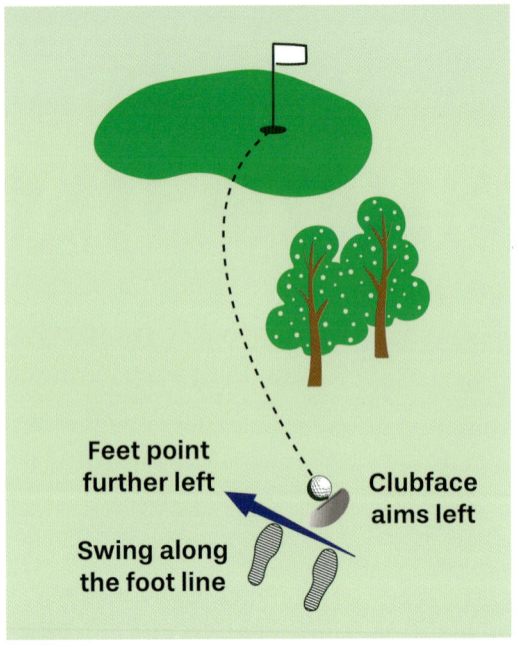

Fading the ball around a tree: you could choose to go either way, but fading is easier than drawing

1. Align your body left of the target and point your clubface right of your alignment at set-up

2. Swing your club along your body alignment (out-to-in) with your clubface pointing to the right of your swing path at impact

3. Swing through to a full finish; your body may point left of your target at the end of the swing; remain in balance

SHOT SHAPING 69

HOW TO DRAW THE BALL

In this case you've decided to draw the ball around the tree:
1. Set the clubface first to send the ball where you want it to start, i.e. to the right of the tree
2. Align your feet and body further to the right than the clubface (the tennis equivalent is giving the ball topspin)
3. Swing along the foot line
4. Do cock and release your wrists, but at impact the clubface should be in the same position it had at address

It's as simple as that!

1. Align your body to the right of the target and point your clubface left of your alignment at set-up

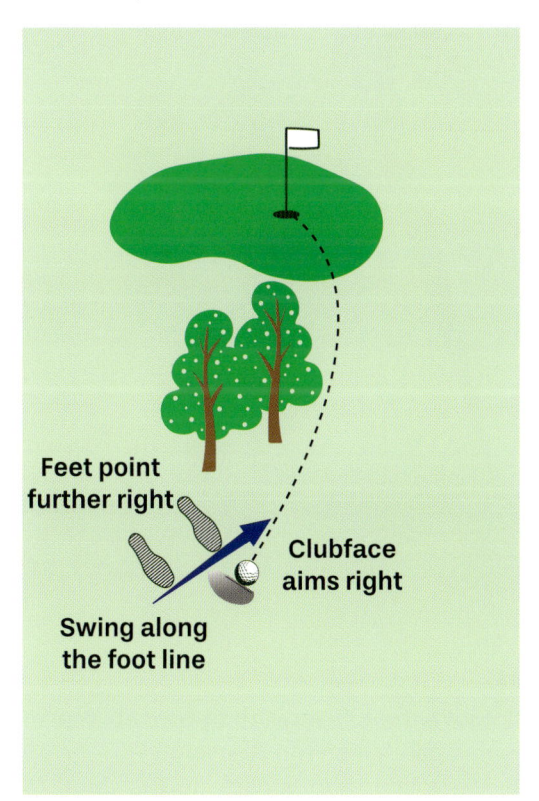

2. Swing your club along your body alignment (in-to-out) with your clubface pointing to the left of your swing path at impact

3. Swing through to a full finish; your body may point right of your target at the end of the swing; remain in balance

Feet point further right
Clubface aims right
Swing along the foot line

Drawing the ball around a tree

VIDEOS
To see a video of Julian demonstrating **shot shaping**, please scan the QR code

In general a draw goes lower than a fade.

If there are hazards bounding the fairway always play your fade or draw so that, if the ball goes straight by mistake, it will miss the hazard (the stream on the left or the wood on the right in the diagram).

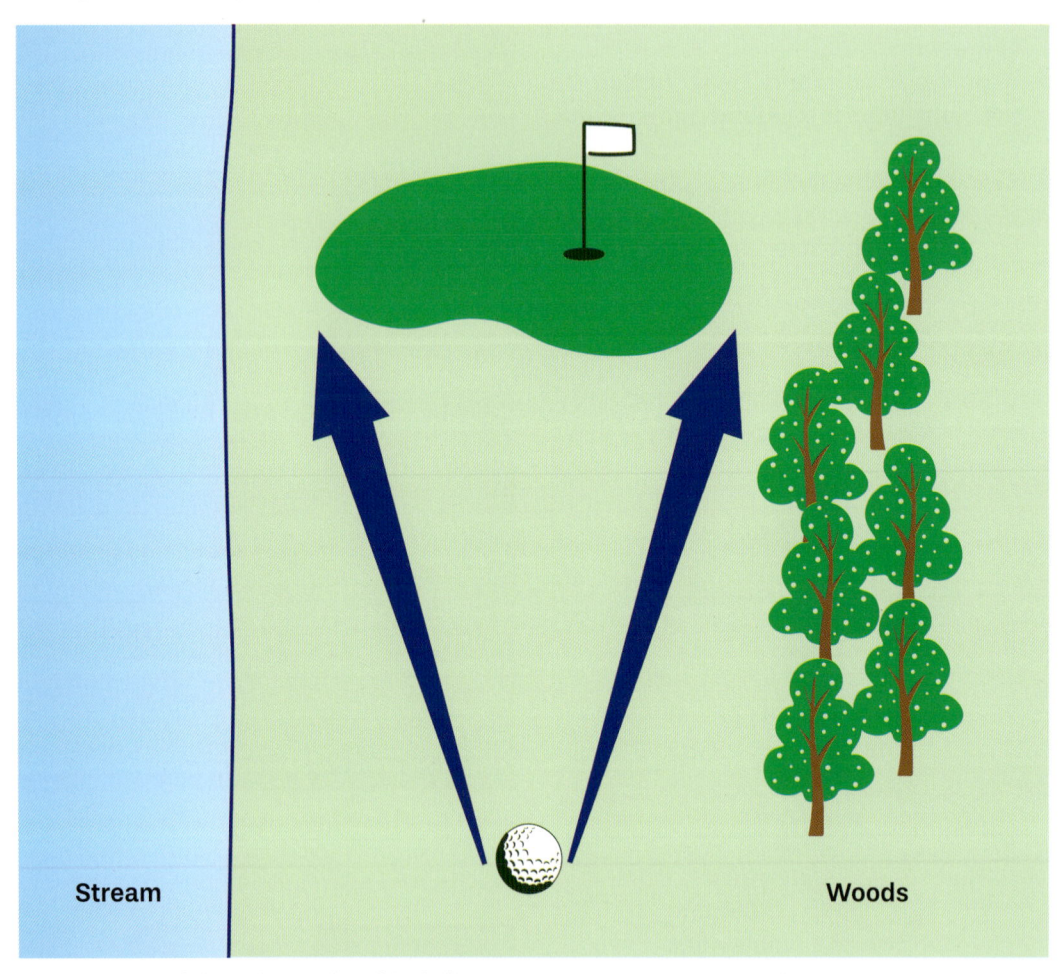

Always play your fade or draw so that, if the ball goes straight, it will miss the hazard

HITTING A HIGH OR A LOW SHOT

This is all about ball position and hand position at address.

To send the ball its normal height you set up with it in the middle of your stance and the club in a neutral position.

To Send The Ball Higher

You ideally need a fluffy lie so the club can get under the ball:

1. Choose your club carefully because the ball will stop quicker than normal
2. Move the ball forward in your stance so you catch it on the upswing
3. Move your hands back (to the right) to give the club more loft. Maintain this angle at impact, and still release the club after impact
4. Your backswing should be more upright as this makes hitting the ball high easier to achieve
5. Swing to a full finish to ensure you carry the ball far enough

SHOT SHAPING 71

Sending The Ball Higher

1. Set up with the ball forwards in your stance; weight either 50-50 or 60-40 on your back foot and point your front shoulder upwards

2. Start the backswing as normal with your arms and club moving together and a gentle weight transfer onto your back foot

3. At hip height cock your wrists upwards as a steeper swing makes this shot a lot easier

4. Finish the backswing having turned and transferred your weight onto your back foot

5. To start your downswing bring the club down more steeply than your normal swing

6. As your hands move past hip height start to release the clubhead to gain the extra height you are looking for

7. Your weight may still be 60-40 on your back foot, fully release the clubhead under the ball with your front shoulder tilted upwards

8. Through impact you may feel the club moving more upwards than back around The Circle; your weight will be moving to your front foot

9. Your finish may feel higher than normal; your body should be facing the target and your weight on your front foot

To Send The Ball Lower

1. Move the ball back in your stance so the club is de-lofted at impact
2. Move your hands forward and keep them there when you make contact. This also de-lofts the club
3. A slightly flatter swing helps hit the ball lower
4. Make sure you move your weight forward through impact to maintain the loft of the club that was set at address
5. It's not uncommon to have a shorter follow-through when playing this shot

VIDEOS
To see videos of Julian demonstrating **shot shaping with high and lows shots**, please scan the QR code

1. Have the ball back in your stance with your hands ahead of it; also raise your hands rather than having them too low at set-up

2. Start the backswing with your weight even between your feet, your arms stay long but relaxed and don't cock your wrists too early

3. Your backswing may feel slightly shorter than normal, and your weight should stay centred

4. Start the downswing with a weight transfer to your front foot to help your body get more in front of the ball at impact

5. At impact keep your hands ahead of the clubhead with the clubface pointing towards the target to de-loft the clubface angle

6. The finish may be shorter than normal; your weight moves onto your front foot and your body faces the target

CHAPTER 8

GETTING OUT OF TROUBLE

The ability to recover is one of the key skills for scoring. We'll look at how to get out of the rough, how to handle difficult locations and how to hit from uneven lies.

PLAYING FROM THE ROUGH

If the ball is in deep rough you can't get far through the grass, so you need to be sensible. You can't hit a wood out of the rough and you need a club with plenty of loft – sometimes even a sand wedge.

- Aim out of trouble and into safety. The grass tends to wrap around the shaft which then twists and closes the clubface, and the shot goes left. So aim right!!
- Set up with the ball in the centre of your stance, not back or you will de-loft the club
- Use a split grip on the handle (no interlocking) to give strength (if required)
- Your intention should always be to **follow through**, though the grass may not let you. So use a steep angle of attack which means you hit less grass on the downstroke. The technique is to **cock your wrists in the backswing** so the shaft goes almost vertical – it's much like a lob shot.

None of us wants to end up in the rough, but occasionally we do!

VIDEOS

To see a video of Julian demonstrating **playing from the rough**, please scan the QR code

Playing From The Rough

1. Use a club with more loft, ball in the middle of your stance and your hands slightly forward of it; weight 50–50

2. Start the backswing with more wrist cock than normal to swing the club more upright

3. Make a full backswing if the shot requires some distance so you can generate extra speed at impact

4. Start the downswing by bringing the club down steeply to avoid hitting too much grass before you strike the ball

5. At impact, fully release your clubhead under the ball to increase the loft to elevate the shot out of the rough

6. Follow though with your weight moving forwards to keep the club accelerating and send the shot the required distance

GETTING OUT OF TROUBLE

LOW & HIGH SHOTS
If you need to make a low or a high shot, these are covered on pages 70-72.

BALL VERY NEAR AN OBSTRUCTION
Ball In Front Of A Tree
Suppose you have hit a very long shot but your reward is to find your ball at the foot of a tree! If the ball is right in front of the tree you may be able to swing diagonally:
- Imagine a line through the ball just clearing the edge of the tree (see diagram)
- Set up with your feet parallel to this line but with the clubface square to the target
- Then swing along the line of your feet

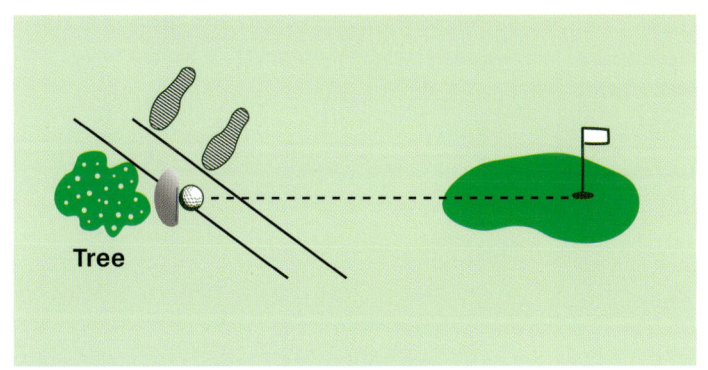

The shot if your ball is in front of a tree

VIDEOS
To see a video of Julian demonstrating **playing a ball in front of a tree**, please scan the QR code

Ball Beside A Tree
If the ball is beside the tree there are two ways of recovering.

In the first method you **face away** from the target with your feet beside the ball (see diagram). You are going to use only your right hand on the club and knock the ball backwards towards the target:
- Stand in an upright posture
- Allow your right arm to hang straight down
- Turn your back to the target
- Face your club towards the target
- You are playing the shot backwards, so swing your arm and club forwards then backwards like a pendulum, striking the ball at the bottom of the arc
- Swing the same length both ways and increase or decrease the speed of the stroke depending on the length of the shot you are attempting

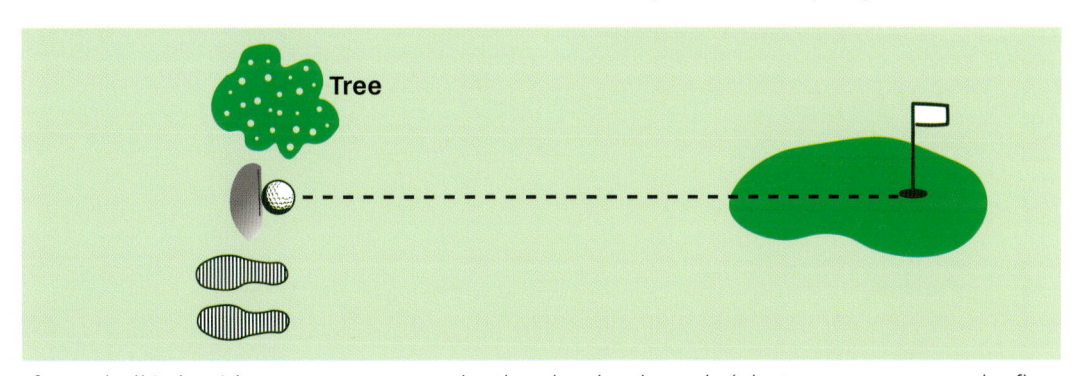

If your ball is beside a tree, you can take the shot backwards (photo sequence overleaf)

Playing A Backwards Shot

1. Face away from the target, body upright, ball opposite your feet; hold the club as an extension of your right arm facing the target

2. Swing the club like a pendulum back and forth, with no need to involve your wrists as you take the club away

3. The length of swing depends on the distance to hit the ball; make sure the club is still an extension of your arm

4. Don't rush the start of the downswing but simply bring it back down on the same path as you took it away on

5. At impact you should be in the same position as at set-up but with the club accelerating

6. After impact, keep the club swinging like a pendulum towards the target to help hit the distance; this shot requires practice

VIDEOS

To see a video of Julian demonstrating **playing a backwards shot by a tree**, please scan the QR code

GETTING OUT OF TROUBLE

An alternative is to **pretend you are a left-handed player**:
- Turn the club around, then grip it with your left hand below your right
- Now make a swing like a leftie ...
- Don't stand too far from the ball and don't try to hit it too far if you've never practised this shot before!

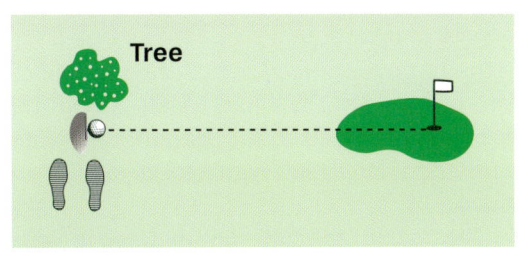

Reverse the club and play like a left-handed golfer

1. Turn the toe of the club upside down pointing towards the target; grip with your left hand below the right; the ball central in your stance

2. Start the backswing by turning your shoulders to move the club away from the ball under control, weight 50–50 between your feet

3. Don't swing the club back too far, especially if you've not tried this shot before, to help keep control of the club

4. Start the downswing smoothly; often the instinct is to hit the ball harder which can be disastrous

5. At impact come back to the set-up position but with momentum and the clubface pointing towards the target; don't try to hit too far

6. Follow through turning your body to the right; transfer your weight forwards keeping the backswing and downswing equal lengths

VIDEOS

To see a video of Julian demonstrating a **left-handed recovery shot**, please scan the QR code

PLAYING FROM A DIVOT

If the bottom of the club hits the top half of the ball the shot will just trickle along the ground. You need to hit the ball below its equator using a club with a lot of loft (7 iron max).

- Set up with the ball slightly back in your stance, allowing for a descending strike to minimise the chance of hitting the edge of the divot
- Shift your weight slightly onto your front foot to ensure a steep angle of attack, helping the club to strike the ball cleanly before reaching the divot
- Swing on a steep plane to avoid hitting the ground too early
- It's essential to shift your weight onto your lead foot through impact
- Emphasise making solid contact with the ball first then the turf – this requires precision and practice
- Don't expect a great outcome because this is a difficult shot, but if it comes out well you've done a great job!

Swing on a steep plane when the ball is in a divot

VIDEOS

To see a video of Julian demonstrating **playing from a divot**, please scan the QR code

1. Place the ball back in your stance, keep your hands forward and your weight slightly forward

2. Cock your wrists early to avoid hitting the back of the divot and making it easier to strike the ball first on the downswing

3. Complete your backswing with your weight 50-50 between your feet

4. Start the downswing with a steep swing and transfer your weight towards the front foot to at least 60-40

5. At impact release your clubhead under the ball to lift it out of the divot with your weight still moving onto the front foot

6. The follow-through may be restricted, but still turn and transfer your weight forward

GETTING OUT OF TROUBLE

BALL AT A DIFFERENT HEIGHT TO YOUR FEET
Ball Above Your Feet

Set up like this:
- Choke down on the grip (holding it lower down) if you like, but it's not essential
- Begin with your spine vertical
- Your arms should be hanging down, touching your chest
- Bend forward from the waist until the club touches the ground
- Shuffle forward until the club addresses the ball
- Aim right because the swing plane is flatter than normal making it easier to close the clubface at impact
- Soften your knees
- **Don't** lean into the slope
- Check your weight is between your toes and heels
- Make a normal or slightly rounded swing
- Try to maintain a balanced finish

VIDEOS
To see a video of Julian demonstrating **playing a ball above his feet**, please scan the QR code

1. Grip down the club slightly if needed; the ball is central in your stance and weight even between toes and heels giving stability; point your body to the right of the target to allow for a draw

2. As you start the backswing your swing may feel flatter than normal because your body is more upright

3. Complete your backswing by turning your hips and shoulders but avoid too much weight transfer onto your back foot

4. Move the club down on the same plane as the backswing for consistent contact with the ball, your weight returning to 50-50

5. Release your club with your weight moving towards the target; it's common for the clubface to be closed making the ball go left

6. Keep turning your body to stop the clubhead overtaking it causing the shot to go too far left; the finish may be shorter than normal

Ball Below Your Feet

Don't bend your knees or 'sit down':
- Start with your spine vertical
- Your arms are hanging down, touching your chest
- Bend forward from the waist until the club touches the ground
- Shuffle forward until the club addresses the ball
- Soften your knees
- Check your weight is between your toes and heels
- Aim slightly left as it's common for the ball to go right
- Make as normal a swing as possible, though it will be more upright
- You will naturally 'come up' on the follow-through

VIDEOS

To see a video of Julian demonstrating **playing a ball below his feet**, please scan the QR code

1. The ball tends to move from left to right so set up to the left of the target; keep the ball central and weight even between toes and heels

2. Your body turn will be restricted: it's ok to feel a more upright backswing rather than a swing that's too flat

3. Complete your backswing as much as possible, maintaining your balance so the start of the downswing is correct

4. Start the downswing moving your arms downwards first, followed by your body turn

5. At impact return to your set-up position in balance, but with the momentum of your body and club moving forwards

6. It's common to see your shot moving left to right: try to maintain balance. The finish may well be shorter than normal

GETTING OUT OF TROUBLE

PLAYING ON A SLOPE
Playing From A Downhill Slope

- The ball will go lower than normal so select a club with more loft
- Bend your uphill (back) knee and keep your spine vertical throughout
- Use your wrists to lift the club on the backswing or it will hit the ground
- Release and follow through on the downswing

VIDEOS
To see a video of Julian demonstrating **playing from a downhill slope**, please scan the QR code

1. Keep your spine upright, your back knee will feel bent and your front leg straighter; place the ball centrally or slightly back

2. Your body turn will be restricted; start the backswing by cocking your wrists more upright than normal to move the clubhead up the slope

3. Complete your backswing but stay stable over the ball and don't move your weight backwards or forwards

4. Start the downswing by moving the club down steeper than normal to help avoid hitting the ground before the ball

5. Release the clubhead so it hits the ball with the correct loft, sending the shot higher; if your hands are too far ahead of the ball the shot will fly very low

6. The finish is often shorter than usual due to the slope, lack of body turn and weight transfer

Playing From An Uphill Slope

Don't have your spine at right angles to the slope. If you do you will get too much loft on the shot, you will probably hit the ground before the ball, and you may lose your balance and make a poor contact. So:
- Bend your top knee so your spine is vertical. (This means the club has its proper loft)
- Your mobility is restricted so you can't make as large a lateral turn as usual. Otherwise aim to make a normal backswing
- Because of the slope the club will tend to hit the ground after impact, so allow both arms to fold after the ball is hit
- Make a balanced finish with your weight on the top leg

You may need to aim a bit right. (The ball tends to draw because, if your weight moves back, the clubface closes quicker than usual.)

VIDEOS
To see a video of Julian demonstrating **playing from an uphill slope**, please scan the QR code

1. Have the ball central in your stance, avoid leaning backwards but keep your spine more upright – your legs will adjust naturally

2. Your body turn will be compromised and balance will be affected but start your backswing as normal; stability is key

3. Complete your backswing with your weight still centred and your balance maintained

4. Start the downswing by bringing the club down towards the ball and avoid leaning backwards

5. Release your clubhead back to the set-up position to present the correct loft to the ball; your weight should be centred and balanced

6. You are more likely to strike the ground just past impact; in this case your finish will be restricted and shorter than normal

CHAPTER 9

COURSE MANAGEMENT

Before you begin a game you should have a plan for each hole, shot by shot. Many golfers do this from the tee to the green but it's better to make the plan backwards from the green to the tee.

To make the plan you will need:
- A yardage chart for each club in your bag, and an idea of your confidence for each club
- To know the par for each hole, and to modify that par for your handicap
- To look at the geography of each hole
- To understand where you should tee up relative to the tee markers

YARDAGE FOR EACH CLUB & ITS CONFIDENCE LEVEL

Your first task is to find how far each club hits the ball. The easiest way to do this is to find a driving range with electronic technology (e.g. Trackman) and spend an hour there. Hit five shots with a club and note how far in yards each ball goes. Averaging this gives you the figure you need – the computer may even do this for you. Repeat for all the clubs in your bag.

The chart shows the sort of results you might find for a golfer with a lower handicap and for one with a high handicap.

Club	Lower handicap golfer	High handicap golfer
SW	80	40
PW	100	70
9	130	80
8	140	90
7	150	100
6	160	110
5	170	120
Hybrid	180	130
5 wood	190	140
3 wood	200	150
Driver	200+	160

Yardage chart for a golfer with a lower handicap and a high handicap (Yardages are a guide for demonstration purposes)

These are yardages for the ball's carry – from take-off to landing. This is very useful when you need to get over a bunker. You may also be able to record the total distance the ball travels – carry plus roll.

You will need one chart for the summer and another for the winter, when each club goes about 15% shorter.

Next, think about how confident you are with each club. Never have a club in your bag that you don't love! For example, take your 5 and 6 irons out of the bag if you hate them and never use them.

The idea is to play to your strengths and work out your strategy accordingly. You may find, for example, that you go haywire with 80-yard (73m) shots to the green. Acknowledge this and organise the way you play so you never leave yourself 80 yards (73m) from the green.

REWRITING THE PAR FOR EACH HOLE

75 percent of golfers take about 100 shots per round, or more, and hardly ever get a par. So for them having par as a hole target is unrealistic. I like to think of a 'New Par' which allows for a golfer's handicap. This builds confidence which means the player is more relaxed and plays better golf.

So if your handicap is 18, for example, you get one extra shot per hole and your 'New Pars' look like this:

Actual par	New par	Shots to green	Putts
3	3 + 1 = 4	2	2
4	4 + 1 = 5	3	2
5	5 + 1 = 6	4	2

That's realistic and a much more positive way of thinking.

For someone with a handicap of 28 the maths is a bit more complicated.

The card of the course has a Stroke Index (S.I.) for each hole. This is a measure of difficulty, from S.I. 1 for the hardest hole to S.I. 18 for the easiest.

The 28 handicapper will get 1 stroke on all the holes plus a further stroke on those with S.I. 1–10 (18 + 10 = 28). It makes sense to have the extra strokes on the hardest holes.

For example, if hole 16 is a par 4 with S.I. 5 this golfer gets two additional strokes and the 'New Par' is 6.

Actual par	Stroke Index (S.I.)	New par	Shots to green	Putts
3	11–18	3 + 1 = 4	2	2
3	1–10	3 + 2 = 5	3	2
4	11–18	4 + 1 = 5	3	2
4	1–10	4 + 2 = 6	4	2
5	11–18	5 + 1 = 6	4	2
5	1–10	5 + 2 = 7	5	2

COURSE MANAGEMENT | 85

If hole 17 is a 321-yard (293m) par 4 and the S.I. is 13 they get one stroke and their 'New Par' is 5. That's 3 strokes to the green and two putts.

Now let's take this example further and see how they might plan the hole. They might hit their driver 160 yards (146m), then their hybrid 130 yards (119m) leaving a 31-yard (28m) chip or pitch to the hole.

Alternatively, they could take two hybrid shots of 130 yards (119m) each, followed by a 61-yard (55m) pitch.

There are lots of options they could take (see the diagram) and they will want to choose the one that gives them the most confidence.

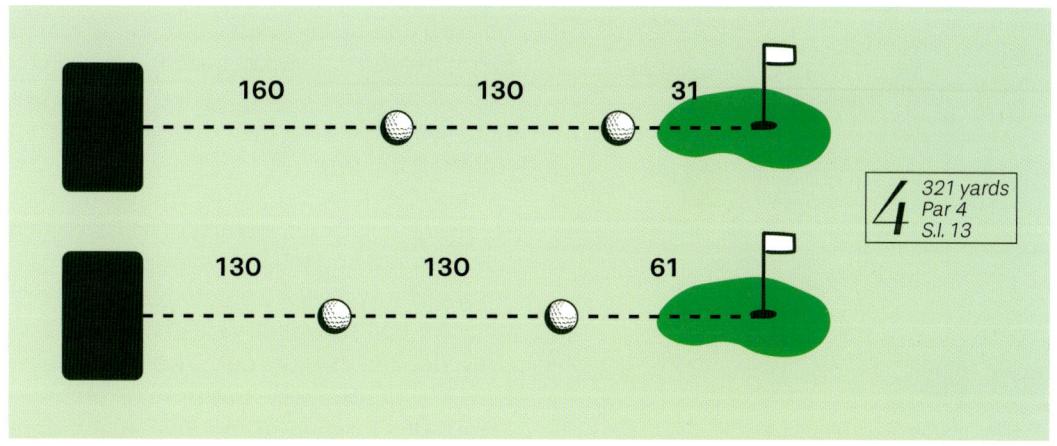

Plan your shots so you play to your strengths: here are two alternative approaches

Note that yardages are given to the centre of the green, but the flag may not be in the centre. If you want to play safe, go for the centre anyway and use the yardage. If you decide to go for the flag adjust the distance accordingly.

PLAYING A HOLE

Many golfers whack the ball off the tee in the hope of hitting the middle of the fairway, then make a plan from there. But down the middle is not necessarily the best strategy. For the hole shown in the diagram below you want to approach the green from the left to avoid going over the bunker. You've worked out you have three shots to the green so play them down the left side of the fairway.

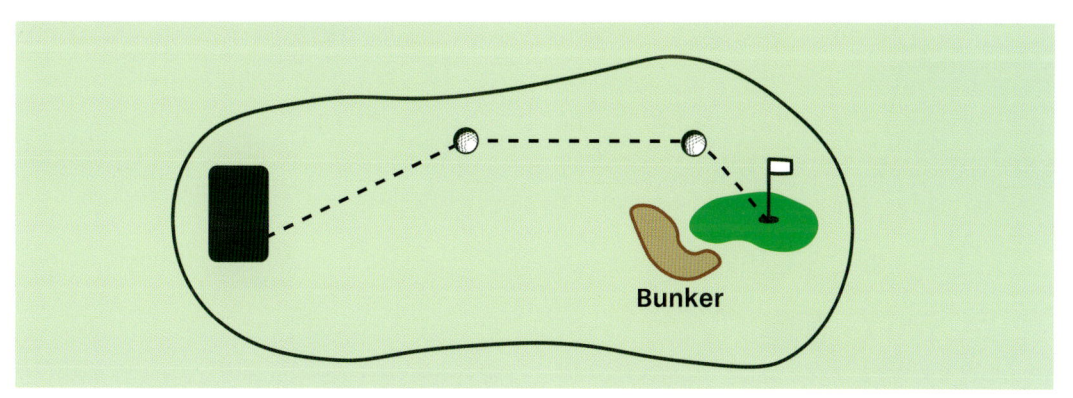

Go left to avoid coming in over the bunker

The next example has a dogleg right. An expert might take the direct route but will need to consider the height of the trees. A high handicapper with three shots to the green would do best to go left and keep round the outside of the bend. Even if they top the final shot it might well roll onto the green!

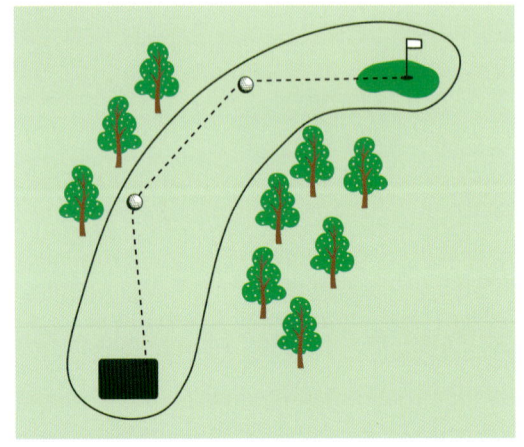

For safety go round the outside of the corner

The following example has a ditch across the fairway. Your drive goes 160 yards (146m) leaving 120 yards (110m) to the ditch. And it's a further 120 yards (110m) to the green. How should you play your second shot?

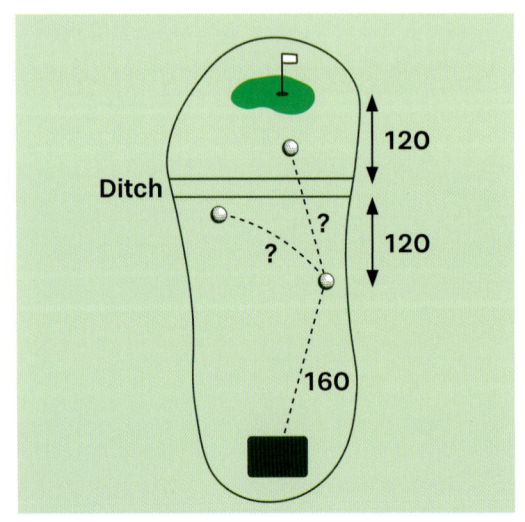

Handling a ditch

As always, the first thing is to avoid the hazard. (The second thing is to consider the pin position.) If you are confident of clearing the ditch with, say, your 5 wood – go for it. Otherwise you may want to lay up, taking a suitable iron. And hitting that iron to the left may be a bit safer in case the ball runs on.

In our final example the golfer has hooked their drive left, and is 40 yards (37m) behind a very tall tree. There are still 250 yards (229m) to go. Their options are to try a miracle shot over the tree, or to chip out from the tree.

They elect to 'Go for it', muttering that trees are mostly air anyway! The ball hits a solid branch and falls down beside the tree trunk. They attempt a left-handed pitch and the ball moves 2 yards (1.8m). At last they decide to chip out. Two shots later they are finally on the green, in 6.

You don't have to go for everything! Better to chip under or past the tree in the first place, then take two further shots and be on the green in 4 strokes.

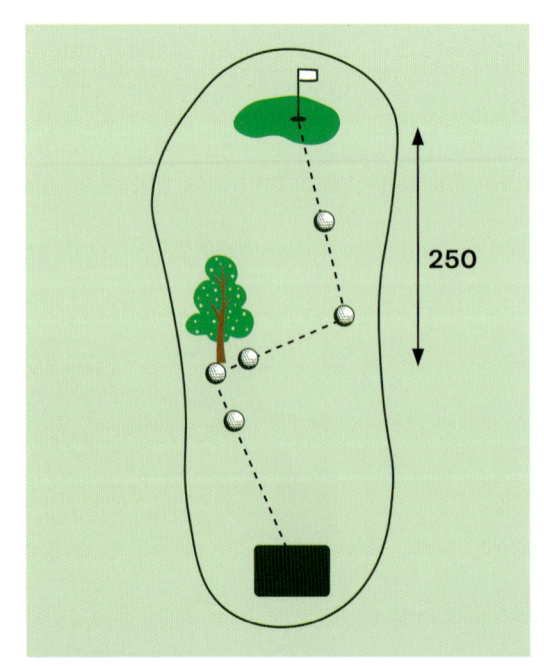

This golfer should have played safe from behind the tree

COURSE MANAGEMENT 87

WHERE TO TEE UP RELATIVE TO THE TEE MARKERS

The tee must be placed within a rectangle two club-lengths in depth, the front and sides of which are defined by the outside limits of the two tee markers. This is the Teeing Ground.

If the Teeing Ground is muddy, move your tee towards the back if that gives a better stance.

If you want the ball to go left (A in the diagram) hit from the right of the Teeing Ground.

If you want the ball to go right (B in the diagram) hit from the left of the Teeing Ground. You can even stand outside the tee marker. It's the ball that has to be in the Teeing Ground.

SUMMARY
- Failing to plan is planning to fail
- 'Hit and Hope' is not a plan
- If you have a plan, your mind is likely to achieve it

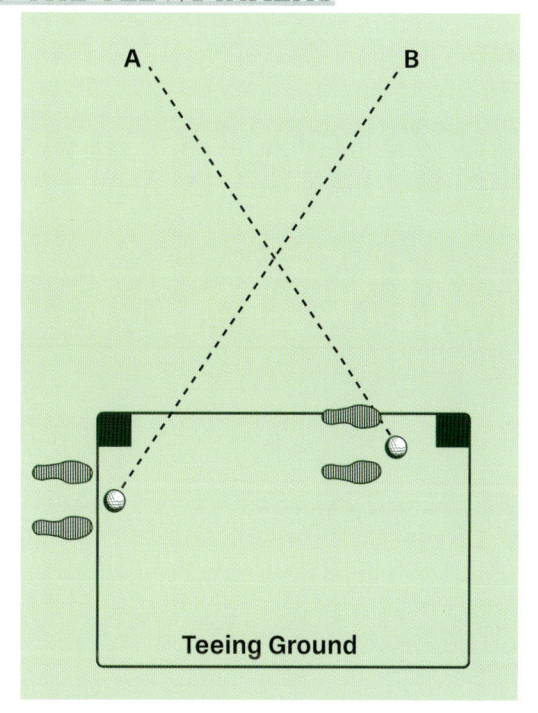

Where to tee up

Have a plan before you start playing a course

CHAPTER 10

THE GOLFER'S MINDSET

In my experience I've found that there seem to be two types of mindset, positive and negative – and not much in between.

In this chapter I'd like to look at both sides and highlight things that people can do if they have a negative mindset and remind those positive mindset people what they do well.

A NEGATIVE MINDSET

Let's take a look at a negative mindset first. Take time to assess your own thoughts when playing well and consider the difference when playing poorly. Don't let a negative mindset define you, remember you are good at things others find difficult.

Just because you struggle with certain things on a golf course doesn't mean you are a negative person.

Here are a few negative traits to consider:

THE GOLFER'S MINDSET

Self-doubt or negative self-talk	Self-doubting golfers often question their abilities, make poor decisions on the course and hesitate during their shots.
Fear of failure	The fear of failure is common and often leads to a build-up of physical and mental tension.
Frustration & anger	Frustration and anger show up either externally or internally depending on their personality.
Dwelling on mistakes	Dwelling on mistakes leads to replaying errors over and over in the head.
Comparing yourself to others	Comparing yourself to others often leads to a feeling of inadequacy, results in a loss of confidence and erodes self-esteem.
Anxiety & tension	Anxiety is a major problem for golfers and that might come from being faced with a difficult shot, first tee nerves or fear of the outcome.
Lack of resilience	A lack of resilience can come from past experiences, external interference or seeing an obstacle as insurmountable.
Perfectionism	You will never be perfect. Trying to be perfect puts extra pressure on you which leads to a negative mindset.
Over-emphasis on results	If you cannot accept a poor result this leads to physical and mental tension – the enemies of a good golf swing.
Feeling isolated or alone	If you are doing your best but not getting the results this leads to depression and anxiety.

I've seen these traits all too often in good players – they have reached a standard that most of us will never attain and yet they are never happy!

A POSITIVE MINDSET

Now, let's compare these to a positive mindset. We've all played with that person who never seems to get ruffled – they are relaxed and exude confidence. So what's their secret? They are commonly optimistic, they lean towards a learning mindset, they stay focused, are single minded, follow a process, have emotional control, are supportive in nature, adaptable, resilient and set themselves goals.

Do any of these things remind you of yourself or somebody you know? Playing with golfers who possess these attributes can either be intimidating or inspirational. They make the game look easy and are generally nice to be with. It's very common for golfers to raise their game in their company and that seems to be by osmosis. So let's look at ways to achieve a positive mindset.

Positive Self-Talk

Replace self-critical statements with affirmations that reinforce confidence and self-belief. That could be something like "I can do this, I love being out on the course, this is my time, the practice I've done is working" or "That's so easy, I will hit the ball over the water, bunkers are a piece of cake."

Self-Awareness

That could be as simple as recognising the words you choose to describe a shot or your swing. Or your body language – have you ever seen somebody winning a tournament and coming up the last in a slouched posture? No, they will have their head up, shoulders back and a broad smile.

Anger adds no value to you on the course – if you hit a bad shot, let it go. Easier said than done I hear you say but practise letting go and before you know it, you'll stop reacting and cherish the challenge of the next shot. Be that nice person to play with, not the one who complains when somebody moves a muscle.

Set Yourself Realistic Goals

Breaking down larger objectives into bite-sized achievable chunks will help you achieve your end goal so much quicker. If something seems unachievable then it probably will be. Celebrate small wins, give yourself a pat on the back when you've executed the shot you intended to play. Listen to positive feedback from your partners and remember that every 1% improvement you achieve is a victory.

Focus On The Process

Swap your focus from the outcome to the process that will get you there. Create a perfect pre-shot routine that works for you and is repeatable. Concentrate on executing each shot to the best of your ability rather than fixating on the final score.

Focus on the process, not the outcome

Visualisation Techniques

Use the power of your mind and visualisation. Picture yourself making a perfect swing, see the shot flying towards your target, imagine what the swing feels like and the satisfaction of pulling it off when it really matters. You can visualise on and off the course. Never underestimate this as it will become the 15th club in your bag.

Resilience

A golfer with a positive mindset exhibits resilience: they bounce back from setbacks and bad shots and stay positive. They don't dwell on mistakes and look forward to a challenge. Remember, you are stronger than you think you are.

Be Adaptable

We all know that best-made plans go astray. The wind may be in a totally different direction from last time you played, the greens could be firm this time when last time you played they were soft. Play aggressively when required but smart when faced with a challenge. To play the course the same way every time you go out is not being adaptable.

Gratitude

Express gratitude for the opportunity to join up in a four ball, be grateful when you get to play while others are working. When a putt is given be grateful but do expect to have to hole out. When you've finished a round and played better than expected don't take it for granted but appreciate everything that you've done to make that happen.

Be Supportive

Congratulating a golfer when they've hit a beautiful shot will always be received well. Seeing your partner sink a putt to halve the hole and congratulating their achievement will give them a well-deserved confidence boost.

Success breeds success, not everything is about you and being that person who applauds someone rather than gloating over their mistakes will ultimately lead to a positive self-mindset.

Be Healthy

This sounds obvious but being healthy is such an integral part of having a positive mindset.

Being mindful about what you eat and drink and taking regular exercise help provide the brain with the essential nutrients it requires to perform to its optimum level. Hydration helps with focus and positivity and feeling fit helps boost your self-esteem.

You have my permission to play as much golf as you can, after all you'll be walking about 5 miles per round. Avoid hopping on a cart if you're able to walk the course.

Be supportive and congratulate a good shot

Stay Optimistic

If your game is suffering a downturn in performance stay optimistic. You have the tools to turn things around and following the techniques in this book will enable you to get back on track sooner than you think.

It's normal to have ups and downs but it's important not to let them affect your future performance.

Stay Relaxed

Getting into a relaxed state and staying there will help with your mindset. Getting angry will automatically affect your thinking and remember: short tight muscles don't move very well.

Be aware of your breathing. Don't sweat the small stuff and allow your subconscious to do its job.

Stay optimistic

SO WHAT CAN YOU DO WHEN IT'S TIME TO PLAY GOLF?

- Begin each round with a positive affirmation and intention
- Focus on what you want to do and not what you don't want to do
- Before the round make sure you are hydrated and have eaten something that gives your body the energy it needs
- Have a plan. This focuses your mind and cuts out the negativity – remember 'failing to plan is planning to fail'
- Play the shot, not the swing. The practice ground is the place to think about your golf swing, on course **play the shot, the swing's for free**

On the journey to the course or in the locker room do some box breathing. Breathe in for 4 seconds, hold your breath for 4 seconds, exhale for 4 seconds, pause for 4 seconds, then repeat. If you've never done this before it may make you feel a bit strange at first but with practice you'll become very good at it. The benefits of box breathing help reduce tension, promote relaxation and enhance focus.

Before you hit your first shot I want you to rehearse your best swing. Imagine how nice that shot will feel. **Pay close attention to your finish**. Science has proven that focusing on your finish can positively impact your performance. It helps with the following features:

THE GOLFER'S MINDSET

The kinetic sequence	Studies have shown that athletes who focus on the finish of their movements tend to exhibit more efficient kinetic sequences. In golf, this means a smoother transition of energy through the body during the swing, leading to improved clubhead speed and accuracy.
Muscle coordination	By concentrating on the finish you'll naturally engage in a more coordinated and fluid swing. This will lead to a more controlled and precise movement.
Visual attention & concentration	Focusing on the finish helps golfers maintain better visual attention throughout the entire swing.
Reducing tension	Aiming for a smooth and balanced finish encourages you to avoid gripping the club too tightly and relaxes the body – this will lead to a much more efficient swing.
Temporal patterning	Scientific studies on motor learning suggest that emphasising the conclusion of a movement helps establish clear temporal patterns in the brain. This can contribute to the development of a well-timed and coordinated swing.
Neurological feedback	Focusing on your finish provides you with immediate sensory feedback about the quality of your swing. This feedback loop can enhance motor learning, which helps you make adjustments for improved movement.
Endpoint	The finish of the swing serves as a natural endpoint, allowing you to set a clear intention of what you want your body to do. The feeling of a solid finish will positively influence your performance on the course. Give your finish a score out of 10. If your finish is poor everything before that will be poor too. Ignore the finish at your peril.

Golf offers way too much spare time to overthink things. It can be the thief of positivity and result in poor performance. Give your brain a job to do rather than let it overthink things.

My challenge to you every time you play is to spot three things on your course that you've never seen before. This stops your overthinking – and what better way to embrace your surroundings and value your environment?

FINAL THOUGHTS ON A POSITIVE MINDSET

Stay calm and give yourself a pat on the back when you've done things well. There is nothing that you can't improve given enough time and patience. Appreciate the fact that you get to play golf and are not stuck down a mine (or whatever).

Life is good when you do things well. Self-confidence and a positive mindset come as a result of achieving your goals. Remember, golf is a game that should be played and is not just a sport. It's a mindful pursuit that fosters camaraderie, personal growth and a profound connection with the nuances of the course.

- Don't mistake being positive for being brave. Smart golf will always beat brave golf
- Set realistic goals for your round based on your current skill level
- Let go of past mistakes, they serve no purpose. Focus on the task ahead without distractions
- If you find yourself standing over the ball with a negative thought, stop and reset. 90% of amateurs won't do this but a 100% of professionals will. It takes a lot longer to find your ball in trouble than it does to reset
- Don't rush. It serves no purpose and builds up unnecessary tension

After Your Round.

Keep a 3-shot diary. Write down in as much detail as possible the best three shots you've hit during the round. Include:
- The course and hole you played
- The club you selected
- The shot you played
- How you felt standing over the ball
- How your swing felt
- The result of the shot
- How it made you feel

This will become the most positive golf book you'll ever read and it can reassure you when doubts arrive.

Re-read this book as often as possible to give yourself positive reinforcement and bolster your confidence.

Be positive

SUMMARY

In conclusion, a positive mindset is the unseen force that transforms your golf game from a mere series of golf swings into a journey of self-discovery and excellence.

When you approach a course with optimism, resilience and focus each shot becomes an opportunity for growth rather than a potential pitfall. A positive mindset not only enhances technical skills but also fosters a deep sense of enjoyment and satisfaction. It allows you to navigate challenges with grace, turning setbacks into stepping stones towards mastery. Ultimately, a positive mindset is the driving force behind a fulfilling and successful golfing experience, shaping not just your game but your entire approach to life.

CHAPTER 11

SENIOR GOLFERS

As golfers age they may experience changes in their bodies that can affect their swing mechanics and overall movement. I have written below about five common problems that senior golfers may encounter and added some suggestions on how to cope with them and continue to play well.

DECREASED FLEXIBILITY

Flexibility tends to decline with age, which can impact a golfer's ability to rotate their body fully during the swing. Limited flexibility can lead to shorter backswings, reduced power and altered swing mechanics.

Here are five exercises that can help improve flexibility as you get older:

Neck Stretches

Gently tilt your head to one side, bringing your ear towards your shoulder. Hold for 15-30 seconds and repeat on the other side.

You can also slowly rotate your head in a clockwise and anticlockwise direction to stretch different neck muscles.

Tilt your head to one side, bringing your ear towards your shoulder

Shoulder Rolls

Stand or sit tall and roll your shoulders in a circular motion. Repeat for 10-15 seconds, then reverse the direction. This exercise helps relieve tension and improves flexibility in the shoulders.

Roll your shoulders in a circular motion

Seated Forward Bend

Sit on the edge of a chair with your feet flat on the floor. Slowly bend forward from your hips, reaching your hands towards your feet or the floor. Hold this position for 15-30 seconds, feeling the stretch in your hamstrings and lower back.

Sit on the edge of a chair and slowly bend forward

Standing Quad Stretch

Stand facing a wall or use a chair for support. Bend one knee and grab your ankle or foot, bringing your heel towards your buttocks. Hold for 15-30 seconds and repeat on the other leg. This exercise targets the quadriceps muscles in the front of your thighs.

Bring your heel towards your buttocks

Calf Stretches

Stand facing a wall with your hands on the wall for support. Step one of your feet back, keeping it straight and pressing the heel into the ground. Lean forward slightly, feeling the stretch in your calf muscle. Hold for 15-30 seconds and repeat on the other leg.

Step one of your feet back from a wall and, keeping it straight and pressing the heel into the ground, lean forwards

LOSS OF STRENGTH

With age, there is often a natural decline in muscle mass and strength. This can affect a golfer's ability to generate clubhead speed and maintain stability throughout the swing.

Here are some simple things you can do to increase muscle strength as you get older:

Resistance Training

Engage in regular resistance training exercises, such as weightlifting or using resistance bands. Start with lighter weights or resistance and gradually increase as you get stronger.

Bodyweight Exercises

Incorporate bodyweight exercises into your routine, such as squats, lunges, push-ups and planks. These exercises use your body weight as resistance and can help improve muscle strength.

Stay Active

Engage in regular physical activity to maintain overall muscle strength and mobility. Walking, swimming and cycling are good.

Balance & Stability Exercises

Include exercises that focus on balance and stability, such as standing on one leg or using a stability ball. These exercises help improve muscle coordination and prevent falls.

Proper Nutrition

Eat a balanced diet that includes sufficient protein and nutrients to support muscle growth and repair. Consult a healthcare professional or registered dietitian for personalised dietary recommendations.

Using resistance bands will help you get stronger

Lunges

Planks

These bodyweight exercises can all help improve muscle strength

A stability ball can help improve balance and stability

Gradual Progression
Gradually increase the intensity, duration or resistance of your exercises over time. This progressive overload helps stimulate muscle growth and strength.

Take Rest Days
Allow your muscles time to recover and repair by incorporating rest days into your workout routine. Rest and recovery are essential for muscle growth and injury prevention.

Stay Hydrated
Drink enough water throughout the day to support muscle function and overall health.

Seek Professional Guidance
Consider working with a fitness professional, such as a personal trainer or physical therapist, who can help design a safe and effective exercise programme tailored to your needs and goals.

JOINT STIFFNESS
As joints age, they can become stiffer and less mobile. This can affect a golfer's range of motion, making it harder to achieve the necessary positions and movements for an efficient swing.

> **TOP TIP**
> Turn your toes out at address to make turning and weight transfer easier.

Here are a few suggestions to help ease stiffness:

Stretching
Incorporate gentle stretching exercises into your daily routine to help improve flexibility and reduce stiffness.

Focus on the areas that feel stiff, which might be your neck, shoulders, back, hips and legs.

Warm-Up
Before engaging in any physical activity or exercise, make sure to warm up your muscles by doing light aerobic exercises or using a heating pad. This helps increase blood flow and loosens up stiff muscles. (See pages 31-32)

Massage
Consider getting a massage or using self-massage techniques like foam rolling to help relax and release tension in stiff muscles.

Self-massage techniques can help relax and release tension in stiff muscles

Heat & Cold Therapy
Applying heat, such as a warm towel or heating pad, can help relax stiff muscles and increase blood flow.

Alternatively, using an ice pack or cold compress can reduce inflammation and numb the area, providing pain relief.

Stay Active
Engaging in regular physical activity and exercise can help maintain joint mobility and prevent stiffness. Choose low-impact activities like swimming, walking or yoga to help keep your muscles and joints flexible.

Hydration
Drink enough water throughout the day to keep your muscles and joints lubricated. Dehydration can contribute to muscle stiffness, so staying hydrated is essential.

Proper Posture
Maintain good posture throughout the day, as poor posture can lead to muscle imbalances and stiffness. Be mindful of your posture when sitting, standing and performing daily activities.

Rest & Recovery
Give your body enough time to rest and recover after physical activity. Over-exertion can lead to muscle stiffness and soreness. Adequate rest allows your muscles to repair and rejuvenate.

BALANCE & COORDINATION
Ageing can sometimes lead to a decline in balance and coordination. This can impact a golfer's stability during the swing, making it more challenging to maintain proper posture and execute a consistent swing motion.

Here are five ways to increase balance and coordination as you get older:

1. Standing On One Leg
Stand near a wall or use a chair for support if needed. Lift one foot off the ground and try to balance on the other leg for 20-30 seconds. Repeat on the other leg. As you progress, challenge yourself by closing your eyes or performing small leg movements while balancing.

Standing on one leg is a great way of improving balance

2. Tai Chi or Yoga
Engage in activities like tai chi or yoga that focus on slow, controlled movements and body awareness. These practices help improve balance, coordination and overall body strength.

3. Balance Exercises
Incorporate specific balance exercises into your routine, such as heel-to-toe walk, tandem stance (standing with one foot directly in front of the other) or standing leg swings. These exercises challenge your balance and improve coordination.

Stand with one foot directly in front of the other to improve balance and coordination

4. Proprioceptive Training
Proprioception refers to your body's ability to sense its position in space. Incorporate exercises that challenge your proprioception, such as standing on an unstable surface like a foam pad or wobble board. These activities help improve balance and coordination by training your body to adapt to different surfaces.

5. Dance or Aerobic Classes
Participate in dance or aerobic classes that involve rhythmic movements and coordination. These activities not only improve balance and coordination but also provide an enjoyable and social exercise experience.

INJURIES & PREVIOUS CONDITIONS

Ongoing or past injuries, such as joint issues, back problems or arthritis can also impact a golfer's movement as they age. These conditions may require modifications to the swing or affect the golfer's overall mobility.

It's important for older golfers to adapt their game to accommodate these age-related changes. This may involve working with a golf instructor or physical therapist to develop a swing that suits their current physical capabilities, focusing on maintaining flexibility, building strength and ensuring proper balance and stability.

Regular exercise, stretching and mobility work can also help mitigate some of the effects of ageing on the body's movement.

To overcome the issues associated with ageing and maintain a good golf game, here are some strategies:

Flexibility & Mobility Exercises

Engage in regular stretching and flexibility exercises to improve range of motion in the joints. Incorporate dynamic warm-up routines before playing or practising to loosen up the body. (See pages 95-96)

Strength Training

Include strength training exercises in your fitness routine to maintain or build muscle strength. Focus on exercises that target the core, back, legs and arms, as these muscles are essential for generating power and stability in the golf swing. (See pages 97-98)

Balance & Coordination Exercises

Incorporate balance and coordination exercises into your fitness regime to improve stability during the swing. Activities like yoga, tai chi, or specific balance drills can help maintain good balance and body control. (See page 99)

Modify Swing Mechanics

Work with a golf instructor who can help you adapt your swing mechanics to accommodate any physical limitations. They can provide guidance on adjustments that optimise your swing while taking into account your body's changing abilities.

Equipment Modifications

Consider using golf equipment designed for older players, such as clubs with more forgiving features or graphite shafts that are lighter and easier to swing.

Regular Practice & Play

Consistency is key to maintaining and improving your golf game. Regularly practise your swing, play rounds of golf and focus on honing your skills and technique.

Listen To Your Body

Pay attention to any discomfort or pain during or after playing golf. If you're experiencing persistent issues, seek advice from a healthcare professional or physical therapist who specialises in sports-related injuries and rehabilitation.

Stay Active & Healthy

Maintain an overall healthy lifestyle by engaging in regular physical activity outside of golf, eating a balanced diet, staying hydrated and getting enough rest and recovery.

Remember, golf is a game for a lifetime. With proper care, adaptation and a positive mindset golfers can continue to enjoy the sport and excel in their game as they age.

CHAPTER 12

FAULTS & FIXES

If you have a consistent fault, for example slicing the ball, this chapter is for you. I'll look at the most common faults and offer remedies for each. And at the end I'll offer some thoughts on what you can do if you suddenly 'lose it' mid-round.

TOPPING THE BALL

If you top the ball everyone says 'You lifted your head'. But it's more likely to be one of four faults:
- Tightening up causes your arm muscles to shorten, which lifts up the club so you hit the top of the ball
- Standing too far from the ball makes you lean forward but during the swing you revert to standing taller and top the ball
- Having your weight on the back foot moves the lowest point of The Circle behind the ball, so the clubface is swinging up by the time it reaches the ball and tops it
- The ball position could be too far back or too far forward in your stance

(Remember that you should allow your head to begin following the ball from a point just before contact – keeping your head down after that stops you following through.)

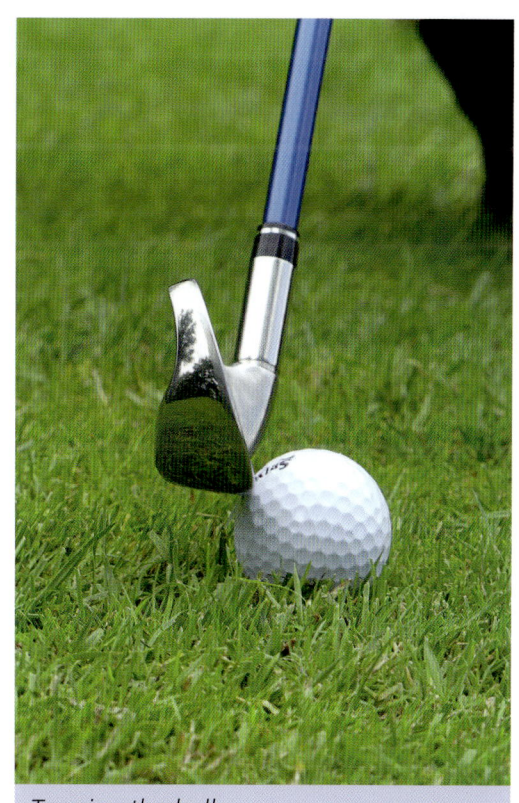

Topping the ball

HITTING BEHIND THE BALL

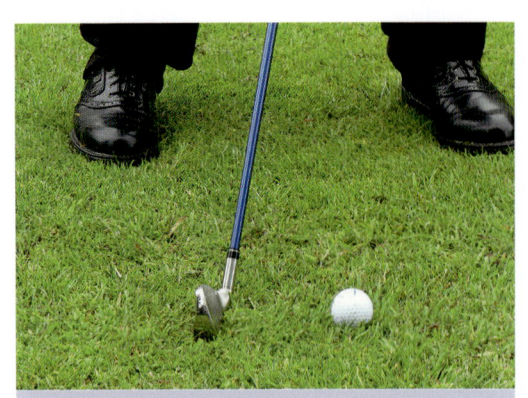

Hitting behind the ball – when you hit the ground before the ball

If you're taking a mighty divot there are three possible problems:
- Your weight is on your back foot and you're leaning back. Make sure you transfer your weight from the back foot to the front and turn correctly
- You are standing too close to the ball at address
- You are lifting the club to the top of the backswing. Keep your arms heavy and initiate the backswing by turning your body, keeping the clubhead low. It feels like you're dragging it along the ground

THE SWING IS TOO UPRIGHT

This swing is too upright

As a rough guide the swing plane should be at about 45 degrees to the vertical. If it's too upright the shot tends to go left and you may hit behind the ball. This could be caused by one of four reasons:
- You are lifting your arms at the beginning of the backswing. Keep your arms heavy and turn your body to initiate the backswing
- You are standing too close to the ball at address
- You are cocking your wrists too quickly at the start of the backswing
- You are shifting your hips laterally to the right in the backswing (which can cause you to lift your arms)

THE SWING IS TOO FLAT

This swing is too flat

If the swing is too flat the ball tends to go to the right, although sometimes to the left:
- A flat swing is due to excessive forearm rotation on the backswing (the back of your left hand points at the sky). This will take the club under The Circle with the clubface very open and if the release doesn't close it the ball shoots right. Although people sometimes over-compensate and release the clubhead too early and too much which hooks the ball left!
- You are standing too far from the ball at address
- You are overemphasising your arms when starting the backswing and not turning your body

FAULTS & FIXES

YOU HOOK THE BALL

A hooked shot

The ball starts to the right then bends viciously left. Usually this is due to the clubface being very closed and the swing too much from in to out. Check your set-up first, then your swing. Here are some possible faults:
- The club is closed at address. Make sure the bottom edge of the club is at right angles to the target line
- You have taken too strong a grip (the palm of your right hand is pointing at the sky)
- You are using excessive forearm rotation in the backswing and follow through
- You have poor weight transfer, i.e. you are keeping your weight on your back foot
- You have a flat swing and are then closing the clubface too quickly at impact
- You are keeping your head down too long after impact
- Your stance is closed at address

YOU SLICE THE BALL

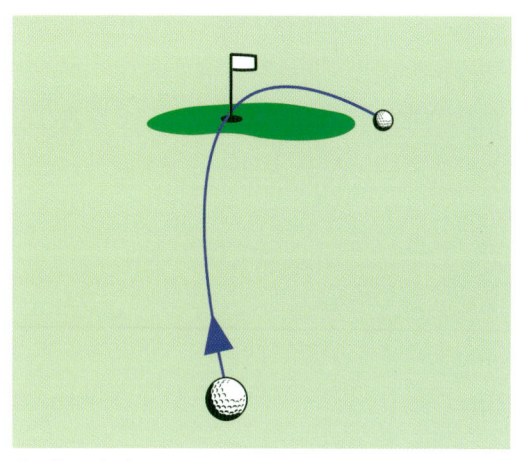

A sliced shot

If the ball bends horribly to the right this is a slice.

The main culprits are an open clubface at impact and an out-to-in swing path, but this has probably been caused by addressing the ball badly. Here are some things to watch:
- Your feet and body are aligned left of the target. Often a slicer will try to compensate by aiming more and more left. This encourages an out-to-in swing path and makes things worse! So make sure you are aligned straight at address
- You are gripping the club too tightly. This hinders the release of your wrists, so the clubface is still open at impact. Grip the club gently
- Your grip is too weak. (The back of your right hand is pointing at the sky.) Once you start the swing the club may rotate, opening the clubface
- The clubface is set open at address. Make sure the bottom of the club is at right angles to the target line
- You are lifting the club too quickly at the start of the backswing
- You are starting the downswing with your shoulders which will cause the club to swing from out-to-in. Start the downswing with your arms

CHICKEN WINGS

Don't let your elbows point out at address

Here your elbows are pointing out at address. You look like you're holding a cannon ball! Your elbows are a hinge joint so it's important that they are set correctly at address, i.e. pointing towards your hips.

Chicken wings cause the ball to go right, with little power.

Usually chicken wings on the follow-through are caused by keeping the head down too long which stops the body rotating, leaving the arms with no room to move into. Chicken wings are often a sign of a fault, not the fault itself. To correct the problem:
- Hold your hands straight out and forwards, palms up. Now turn your wrists so your hands touch and make your normal grip. This is the set-up you want
- At the top of the backswing feel that your elbows are pointing down, not out
- Three-quarters of the way through the follow-through feel that your elbows are pointing down, not out to the side

OVER-THE-TOP DOWNSWING

Don't let your shoulder go down and left at the beginning of the downswing – the shoulders should be rotating around the spine

At the beginning of the downswing the left shoulder goes down and left, whereas the shoulders should be rotating around the spine.
- One cure is to imagine the left shoulder going up on the downswing
- Check your set-up to make sure your shoulders are not pointing too far left. This is a common fault with the driver because the ball position is further forward than normal
- Lack of hip turn in the backswing can lead to the upper body being dominant in the downswing
- Make sure you transfer your weight on the downswing from the back foot to the front foot
- Keeping your head down can influence the swing path and lead to an over-the-top downswing
- Too much tension in the hands, arms and shoulders can ruin the fluidity of the swing
- Avoid the hit instinct at the start of the downswing. (Remember, the fastest part of the swing should be just **after** impact)

YOU HAVE NO POWER

You need to increase your clubhead speed. (One leading professional has been measured with a swing speed of 122mph and a ball speed of 183mph. His average driving distance is over 320 yards [293m].) Here are some suggestions:

- Grip the club loosely. (Tight muscles are really slow.) And make sure you don't have a weak grip (see page 15)
- Sign up for some speed training in the gym. Do a series of short sprints. Throw a medicine ball hard at the floor. Strengthen all parts of your body using weights. (Remember to get professional advice if you are going to embark on this type of training)
- Use a rod or a towel to practise swishing. Or even better swing a Rypstick or a similar training aid. The swish comes from relaxed speed, not from a hitting action. In fact force is usually slower than speed
- Swing to a balanced finish. If you quit on the swing your clubhead speed will drop
- Make sure that you are turning and shifting your weight correctly on the backswing and follow-through
- Check your equipment. After a while steel shafts become stiffer and less flexible which will reduce distance
- Don't quit on your shots. Commit to the distance you want to hit the ball and avoid guiding it as this will reduce your swing speed
- Striking off-centre can have a dramatic effect on distance. Check this by using a clubface sticker or something similar. (Hitting the ball out of the heel has the most dramatic effect on distance)
- Avoid cupping the wrists at impact as this adds loft to the club and reduces distance
- The fastest part of the swing is just after impact, not at the start of the downswing. So avoid the instinct to hit the ball – instead swing the club freely, fluidly and fast

Swing a Rypstick to practise swishing

VIDEOS

To see a video of Julian demonstrating **using a Rypstick to practise swishing**, please scan the QR code

SKYING THE BALL
Sometimes a shot from a wood or driver goes very high. Either the club has gone under the ball, or the club has chopped down on it.
- Check your tee height. With the driver on the ground the top of the driver should be no lower than the ball's equator (see page 34)
- Don't pick up the club on the backswing. Begin by turning your body, almost dragging the club back
- Don't swing 'over the top'. Begin the downswing with your arms, not your shoulders
- Check that your ball position is not too far back at address
- Check your alignment. Often the stance and shoulders are open to the target which causes an in-to-out swing path

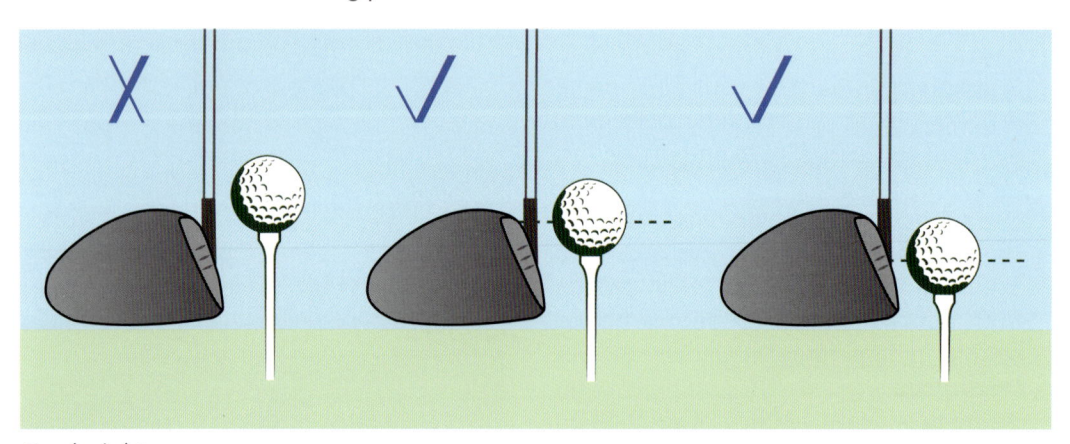

Tee height

SLASHING AT THE BALL
Golfers who slice the ball are often described as 'slashing at the ball'.
Here are some possible cures:
- Think about swinging the club, not hitting with it
- Set up with your shoulders square to the target. Relax your shoulders
- Concentrate on turning your body correctly and not just using your arms
- Swing around The Circle, don't cut across it
- Release your wrists
- Don't try to hit the ball too hard, which often leads to a slashing action. When this happens you tend to grip the club too tightly which stops you swinging the clubhead freely
- Start the downswing with your arms. If you start with your shoulders this causes an over-the-top swing

MISS-HITTING A CHIP SHOT
As aways, first check your set-up. Then:
- Don't swing on a plane that is too flat. With a short shaft The Circle should be more upright than with a longer club
- There should be a gentle transfer of weight to your front foot. If your weight stays on your back foot the club will hit the ground
- Try not to use your wrists to lift the ball at impact. You will either hit the ground before the ball or the bottom leading edge of the club will hit the middle of the ball and top it
- Relax. Too much tension leads to a poor chipping action
- Stand square to the ball. Your stance shouldn't be too open
- Check the shaft lean at address. Your hands shouldn't be in front of the clubhead

YOU LOSE IT – YOU CAN'T HIT THE BALL!

Occasionally, mid-round, you hit one bad shot after another.

Or you may even freeze over the ball. You feel that you've 'lost it'.

Don't panic! You need to reset.

There are two main problems:
1. In golf you have a lot of time between shots which gives your mind the opportunity to become cluttered with swing thoughts
2. Because the ball doesn't move your instinct is to hit it, not swing through it

What we're after is to clear your mind and to swing freely.

Here are some things you can do to reset:
- Check your set-up. People get comfortable with an incorrect set-up and revert to it when under pressure. Remember: Grip. Arms. Bend forward from the Hips. Soften the Knees. (See pages 18-19)
- Reduce tension. Squeeze the club, then relax
- Put your swing thoughts to one side. You need to get back the feeling of a good swing, not a thought. Remember how it felt to swing the towel? Make a few continuous swings with your club that feel like that

If time allows try this exercise:
- Standing upright, make five continuous swings around the body. Feel the clubhead swinging, feel your wrists cocking and releasing, feel your body turning, feel the shaft hitting your shoulder on the follow-through. Any faults are highlighted in this mode and are easily recognised
- Now lean forward slightly and swing five times around this arc
- Lean forward a bit more, but still with the clubhead above the ground, and swing five times on this steeper arc

Once you have the good feeling back, you're ready to play your shot.

A FINAL THOUGHT

Let me finish with a personal anecdote.

I used to be an angry golfer – I just couldn't bear to play bad shots or make mistakes. One day I really lost it in front of another player's coach.

He watched me throw my club on the ground and curse the course, the game of golf and everyone who plays it. He let me finish, then came over and gave me the best piece of advice I've ever been given.

"Julian, we're not good enough to get angry. But with an open mind and curiosity everyone can improve. DON'T GET ANGRY, GET CURIOUS."

I'll leave you with that thought and this book to help you transform your game.

VIDEOS

To see a video of Julian talking about **not getting mad, but getting curious**, please scan the QR code

APPENDIX

PARTS OF A GOLF CLUB

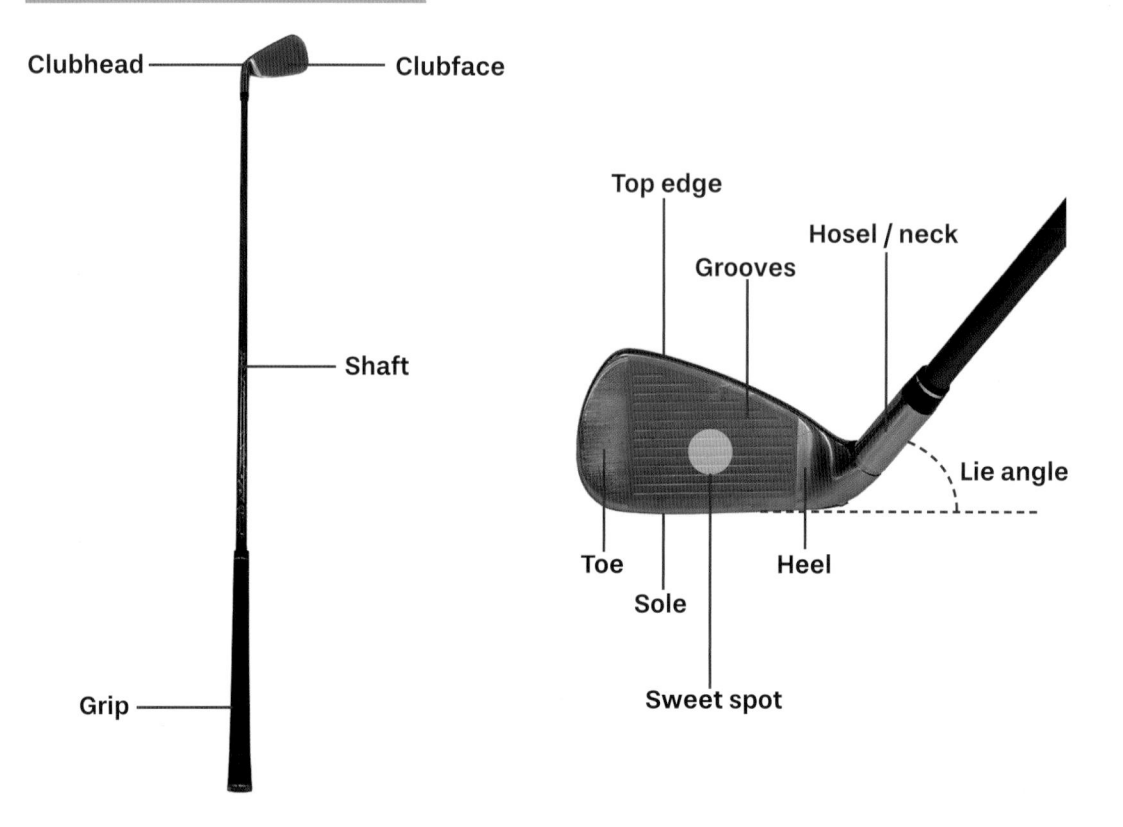

Clubhead — Clubface

Shaft

Grip

Top edge
Grooves
Hosel / neck
Toe
Sole
Heel
Sweet spot
Lie angle

APPENDIX

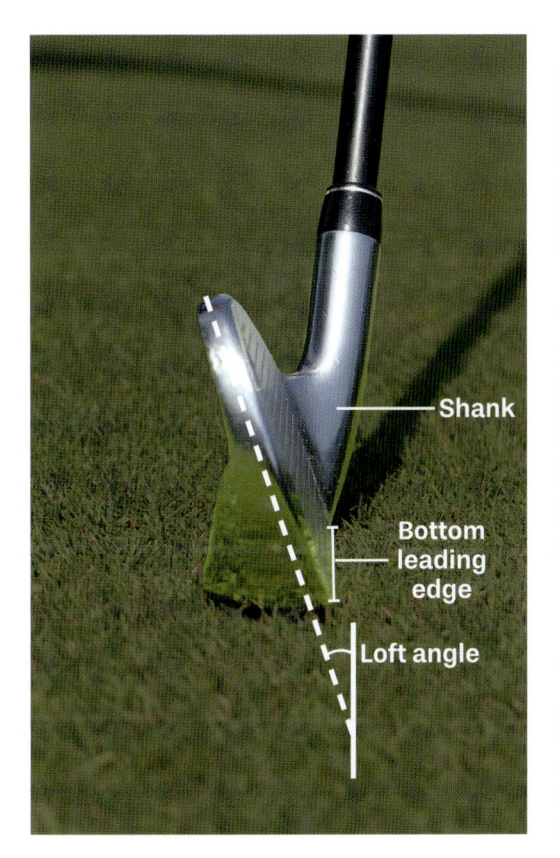

Labels on images: Shank, Bottom leading edge, Loft angle, Bounce, Bounce angle

TYPES OF GOLF CLUB

Name	Description / Use
Driver	The club designed for maximum distance off the tee: it has the longest shaft and the largest head
Fairway wood	Distance clubs: drivers and fairway clubs
Hybrid	A club designed to be between an iron and a wood
Iron	A club designed for accuracy and control on shorter shots from the fairway, rough or tee; they are numbered (1-9) to indicate different loft angles and shaft lengths
Wedge	A specialised club with a high loft designed for short-distance, high shots; typically used for approach shots near the green or shots out of bunkers
Putter	A club used on the green to direct the ball to the hole

GLOSSARY

Address	Set-up when preparing to make a shot
Backspin	Backward rotation of the ball; the spin and trajectory make the ball stop quickly or spin backwards
Backswing	The initial part of the swing moving the club away from the ball
Ball position	Position of the ball relative to your feet
Bottom edge	Bottom front edge of the clubface
Bounce	The shape of the bottom edge of the wedges, designed to prevent the club digging into the ground / sand too much
Break	The shape of the green
Carry	Distance from connection to landing
Chip	A shot to the green which rolls more than it carries
Circle	The path of the clubhead
Closed	Body: points right. Clubface: points left
Clubface	The part of the club that hits the ball
Clubhead	The club excluding the shaft and grip
Cock your wrists	Rotate the wrists upwards creating an angle between the shaft and forearms (enabling power generation and control during the swing)
Downswing	The part of the swing from the top of the backswing to the ball
Draw	A shot that starts right of target and curves left to finish on target
Fade	A shot that starts left of target and curves right to finish on target
Fairway	The closely mown area of the course that lies between the tee box and the putting green
Follow-through	The part of the swing from the ball to the finish
Grip	Hands: form a grip around the club. Club: the part of the club you hold
Heel	Where the club shaft joins the clubhead
Hole out	To get the ball in the hole
Hosel	See 'Neck'
Interlocking grip	Index finger of left hand and little finger of right hand interlink
Lie	Angle between the shaft and the bottom leading edge of a golf club. The term is also used to describe the way the ball is sitting on the ground
Lob	High shot that stops quickly, played from close to the green
Loft	Angle of the clubface to the vertical
Neck	Where the club shaft joins the clubhead (also Hosel)
Open	Clubface pointing right

Overlap grip	Little finger of right hand fits into gap between index finger and middle finger of left hand
Pitch	Short shot that carries further than it rolls
Pull (a shot)	The shot starts left of target and curves further left
Release	The wrists cock in the backswing then uncock (release downwards) in the downswing, giving power and clubhead speed through impact
Rough	Long grass
Shaft	Connects the grip to the head of a golf club
Slash	A shot when the club strikes down sharply on the ball, giving a low, skidding trajectory
Slice	A shot that starts left of the target and curves to the right of it
Split-hand grip	Hands are separated
Square	The clubface at 90 degrees to the target line
Stance	Where your feet are at address
Strong grip	Hands turned clockwise on the grip
Sweet spot	The middle of the clubface
Swish	The noise a fast-moving club makes on the downswing
Target	Where you want the ball to finish
Target line	The imaginary straight line from the ball to your intended target
Top edge	Upper edge of the clubface
Weak grip	Hands turned anticlockwise on the grip

FERNHURST
BOOKS

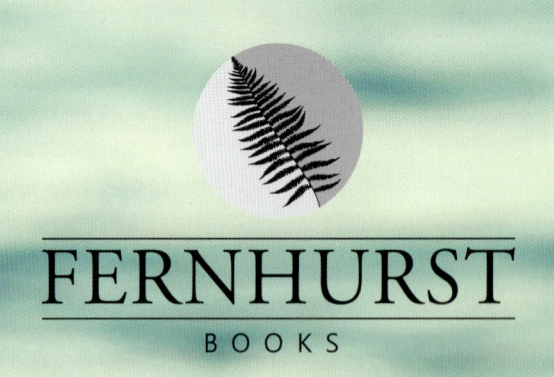

We hope you enjoyed this book

If you did, **please post a review on Amazon**

Discover more books on

SAILING • RACING • CRUISING • MOTOR BOATING

SWIMMING • DIVING • SURFING

PADDLING • FISHING • SKIING • GOLFING

View our full range of titles at www.fernhurstbooks.com

Sign up to receive details of new books & exclusive special offers at

www.fernhurstbooks.com/register

Get to know us more on **social media**